I Wish I TALKED TO YOU SOONER

Advance Praise for *I Wish I Talked To You Sooner*

"Too often, families put off conversations about estate planning until life becomes more complicated. *I Wish I Talked To You Sooner* reminds readers that estate planning is about much more than legal documents. It is about protecting the people we love, communicating our wishes, and making the future a little easier for those we care about. Written in clear, approachable language, this book offers practical guidance that helps families prepare with confidence, clarity, and peace of mind."

—**Megan McCoy**, Ph.D., LMFT, AFC®, CFT™,
Associate Professor Personal Financial Planning,
Kansas State University

"*I Wish I Talked To You Sooner* transforms estate planning from an intimidating legal exercise into an act of love and responsibility. With clarity, compassion, and practical wisdom, Ilya Lyubimskiy guides readers through the decisions that matter most, helping families avoid unnecessary stress, conflict, and uncertainty when it matters most."

—**Martin M. Shenkman**, CPA, MBA, JD, PFS, AEP (Distinguished)
is author of more than 40 books and more than
1,400 articles on estate planning and related topics

"As someone who has spent nearly two decades helping people break the silence around money, I know that the most loving thing you can do for your family isn't leaving them a perfectly drafted estate plan; it's talking to them about it before you're gone. *I Wish I Talked To You Sooner* is the practical guide to estate planning that helps families break money silence before it's too late."

—**Kathleen Burns Kingsbury,** author of *Breaking Money Silence*

"I've spent years helping families deal with what happens after someone they love is gone, and I've learned that the greatest gift we can leave behind isn't just documents—it's clarity. In *I Wish I Talked To You Sooner*, Ilya Lyubimskiy gives families exactly that. His practical, compassionate guidance will help readers avoid unnecessary confusion, reduce stress for the people they love, and finally act before it's too late. This is a book every family should have on their shelf."

—**Jon Braddock**, Co-Founder & CEO, My Life & Wishes,
Creator of The Legacy Vault™

"With the death of both my father and brother, I saw the best and, unfortunately, the worst of estate planning. Estate planning isn't an easy 'have one' or 'don't have one' measurement. A complicated and poorly thought-out plan is worse than no plan. I'm so grateful that this book provides a roadmap to the best ideas. I thought a will and financial planning were all I needed. Now I know that is just the start, and probably not even the right start. Read this book and avoid the mistakes one of my family members made."

—**Tom Searcy**, bestselling author of
How To Close A Deal Like Warren Buffett

"*I Wish I Talked To You Sooner* is exactly what financial grownups need to make sure those they love are protected and taken care of in the future. Ilya Lyubimskiy takes a topic many people will never feel 'adult' enough to tackle, and makes it approachable, practical, and relevant to real life."

—**Bobbi Rebell**, CFP®, CFT™, author of *How to be a Financial Grownup* and *Launching Financial Grownups*

"As a veteran financial advisor, I've seen firsthand that the challenge of estate planning is not complexity. It's procrastination. People who don't draft a plan won't live to regret it. But their family will! Ilya's plain English will transform good intentions into action. Read this book, then do your estate plan. Don't let 'someday' become a trainwreck for the people you love."

—**L. Paul Dorsey**, CFA, author of *Ditch The Pitch*

"Estate planning can feel overwhelming, which is why so many people put it off. *I Wish I Talked To You Sooner* is a clear and compassionate guide to the planning conversations families too often postpone. Ilya helps readers understand that estate planning is about making life easier for the people who may one day need answers. With practical guidance and plain-English explanations, *I Wish I Talked To You Sooner* helps families avoid preventable mistakes."

—**Abby Schneiderman**, Co-founder of Everplans and Co-Author of *In Case You Get Hit by a Bus*

I Wish I Talked To You SOONER

How To **Avoid**
The Worst **Estate Planning Mistakes**

ILYA LYUBIMSKIY

INDIE BOOKS INTERNATIONAL®

I Wish I Talked To You Sooner

How To Avoid The Worst Estate Planning Mistakes

Printed in the United States of America.

ISBN 13: 978-1-966168-88-1
Library of Congress Control Number: 2026920029

Designed by Melissa Farr, Back Porch Creative, LLC

INDIE BOOKS INTERNATIONAL®, INC.
2511 WOODLANDS WAY
OCEANSIDE, CA 92054
www.indiebooksintl.com

Dedication

In loving memory of my mother, Yelena,
and my grandmother, Aleksandra.
Both of you raised me, loved me, and
lifted me up throughout your lives.
Rest in peace.

Table Of Contents

Preface

Why I Write This Book

recommend third-party websites, services or products. My goal is not to overwhelm you or scare you into decisions. It is to give you clarity, confidence, and a practical road map so you feel empowered to start your own planning. The stories and examples in this book were created for educational purposes. They are inspired by common estate planning issues I have encountered throughout my legal career and do not depict actual people or real-life events.

Reading this book or navigating to resources listed in the book does not create an attorney-client relationship. This book is intended for educational and informational purposes only. If this book helps you start estate planning sooner, update what you already have, or simply feel more prepared, then it will have done its job: smoothing out the bumps in the road and making an already stressful transition easier for the people you love.

Ilya Lyubimskiy, JD, CPA
Denver, Colorado

Check out my free resource library:
https://premierlegacylaw.com/resources/

PART I

Chapter 1

Why An Estate Plan Matters To Those You Love

We should remember that good fortune often happens when opportunity meets with preparation.
—Thomas Edison

Many people already know they should get around to estate planning—right after the next work deadline, the next trip, the next busy season, or simply when the time is right. Too often, our best-laid plans to get our planning done end up in the same mental drawer as starting to work out and organizing the garage. All for later.

But life has a way of interrupting us with a sudden hospital visit, an inpatient surgical procedure, or a car accident that leaves you unable to handle your own busy life for a few weeks. Maybe our time on this earth will run out suddenly. And now a simple question lands with surprising weight: "If something happened to you, what do your loved ones do next?"

In our busy world, our stuff isn't in one place. Instead, we are increasingly online, behind logins, two-factor authentication, employer portals, autopay systems, and accounts at multiple financial institutions and banks you opened years ago and barely think about now. Most families don't think about these considerations until life throws us one of those interruptions.

What People Think Estate Planning Is

When I ask most people what estate planning means to them, I usually hear some version of the same three answers:

"It's about leaving your stuff to your family when you die."

"That's for people with a lot of money."

"I'm too young and healthy to need that."

Those reactions are common—and completely understandable. The phrase *estate planning* itself sounds formal and expensive, as if it is not meant for the everyday person. It also sounds like a topic you only deal with at the very end of life, so it's easy to push it aside and assume it can wait.

But defining it so narrowly is exactly why so many families get caught off guard. I hear these same assumptions from people in every stage of life—young professionals, new parents, retirees, small business owners, and people who swear to me that they don't have an estate. The truth is that most people aren't avoiding estate planning because they don't care. They're avoiding it because they don't realize what it all really covers—or how quickly life can force the issue.

Estate planning is not just about death. It's about control, clarity, and protection when life changes suddenly. And once you understand that the entire subject shifts from morbid paperwork to something far more practical: a way to guide the people you love through a minefield they don't even realize they may have to navigate.

> Estate planning is not just about death. It's about control, clarity, and protection when life changes suddenly.

Estate Planning Is A Plan For Living

Estate planning isn't just about dividing assets someday. It's about protecting yourself and the people you love *right now.*

At its heart, estate planning is the process of organizing your personal, financial, and medical wishes so they're legally recognized and can be carried out if you become incapacitated or pass away. It's about making the big decisions while you're able—so that if life throws a curveball, the people who step in for you aren't guessing, scrambling, or forced into court just to make those decisions without you. A working estate plan names the trusted individuals who can manage your finances, make healthcare decisions, and follow your instructions when you can't make those choices yourself.

Many people still believe estate planning is mainly for wealthy families or for the very end of life. But that view misses the bigger purpose. Estate planning is for anyone who cares what happens to their health, their home, their accounts, their children, and their legacy if they're suddenly unable to handle things personally.

When you look at it that way, estate planning isn't morbid—it's practical. Like insurance, it's not something most people feel excited to buy. But when something unexpected happens, you're grateful it is there for you. It gives you control, it gives your loved ones direction, and it creates peace of mind that the people you trust can act quickly and confidently when it matters most.

And if this kind of planning is as broadly useful as it sounds, the obvious question is: Why do so many people still avoid it? That's what we'll unpack next.

Three Things Every Plan Must Do

When people hear the words "estate plan," they often picture documents—wills, trusts, forms, signatures. But the documents are just the tools. The real question is whether your plan can actually do what it's supposed to do when life gets messy.

A functional estate plan should accomplish three core things—no matter your age, net worth, or family structure.

Keep You In Control During Incapacity

Many planning failures happen while someone is still alive. A sudden accident, a stroke, a complicated surgery, or a cognitive decline can leave a person unable to manage finances or make medical decisions—sometimes temporarily, sometimes permanently. Without the proper legal authority in place, spouses and adult children are often shocked to learn they cannot step in to make decisions automatically.

A strong plan names trusted people who can act for you—pay bills, manage accounts, coordinate benefits, communicate with medical providers, and make decisions consistent with your values. In other words, it protects your life while you're living it.

Transfer What You Own To The Right People, The Right Way

After death, your plan should do more than say who gets what. It should help your loved ones carry out your wishes efficiently and predictably. That includes reducing confusion, minimizing court involvement when possible, and avoiding the kinds of unintended outcomes that happen when beneficiary designations, outdated documents, and family assumptions collide.

A good plan creates a clear path from point A to point B—so your family isn't forced to interpret your intent while they're grieving.

Reduce Conflict And Make It Easier On The People You Love

Even loving families can fracture under stress, ambiguity, and perceived unfairness. A plan that's legally valid but practically unclear can still invite conflict—especially if no one knows where the documents are, who is in charge, or why certain choices were made.

The best plans don't just distribute assets. They distribute clarity. They name decision-makers, set expectations, and reduce the opportunities for misunderstandings that turn grief into resentment.

When an estate plan accomplishes these three things—protection during incapacity, clear transfer after death, and clarity that reduces conflict—it stops being paperwork and becomes something far more meaningful: a framework your loved ones can actually use.

And once you understand that, the next step becomes much simpler: learning which tools accomplish which job, and how they fit together.

Estate planning is an important and everlasting gift you give your family. And setting up a smooth inheritance isn't as hard as you might think.

—Suze Orman

A Wake-Up Call In The Numbers

As of 2025, one major national survey found that only 24 percent of US adults have a will.[1] Yes, you read that correctly. The takeaway is that most adults still haven't put even the basic legal safeguards in place. That means approximately one out of every four adults in the US have recorded their wishes and preferences into a legal document that dictates what happens to their assets after they pass away. The other three out of four American adults haven't put their wishes into a legally binding document.

What makes this more concerning is the trend's direction. That same survey shows the percentage of adults with a will declined from 2022 to 2025, even after the pandemic briefly pushed more people to take planning seriously. The current trend is not good. In 2022, 34 percent of US adults had an estate plan, a figure that had been rising since 2020—partially due to the COVID-19 pandemic.[2] Some people put it off because they assume they don't need it yet or ever, while others believe their situation is too simple to justify recording their wishes formally.

Why the decline? Many people assume they don't have enough to protect or that they'll "get to it later." Yet estate planning isn't a luxury; it's a safeguard against confusion, family turmoil, and needless loss of time and money.

Estate planning is a gift that helps us preserve wealth across generations. Without a will or trust, passing down property can become complicated, spark family conflict, or even lead to the loss of assets. The disparities are stark. An Urban Institute study found that about 35 percent of older white homeowners with children lack a will or trust, compared with nearly 70 percent for Black homeowners and 76 percent for Hispanic homeowners.[3] That gap leaves millions of families—especially households of color—more vulnerable to delays, legal fees, and fractured inheritances.

Numbers like these are more than statistics; they're a mirror reflecting how uneven access to legal planning widens the wealth gap. Each unplanned estate leaves loved ones facing the hardest moments of loss and grief, while also trying to navigate complex legal and financial steps with no clear road map.

Here's the part most people don't realize—not having an estate plan doesn't mean nothing happens. It means you've handed the decision-making to your state's default rules. If you become incapacitated or you die without clear legal instructions, state law tells us who can manage your finances, make medical decisions, handle your affairs, and inherit your property. That process often runs through the court system—not because your family did anything wrong, but because the law requires a structure when you didn't choose one.

Planning ahead keeps you in control. It lets you decide who steps in, what happens, and how smoothly your loved ones can move through an already difficult time—without having to navigate a legal maze while they're grieving.

> Estate planning isn't a luxury;
> it's a safeguard against confusion,
> family turmoil, and needless loss of time
> and money.

Chapter 2

Don't Fall Into The Putting-It-Off Trap

Procrastination is the thief of time.
—Edward Young

If estate planning is so important, why do so many people avoid it? It's not because they're careless. It's because estate planning sits at the intersection of three things humans are wired to resist: discomfort, complexity, and uncertainty. Even mentioning the possibility of incapacity and death can feel uncomfortable. In fact, studies have shown that we tend not to think about the future as much in part because of how our brains are wired.[4] Here are some of the reasons we put off planning:

- We assume tomorrow is guaranteed. Most of us don't consciously think, "I might be incapacitated next month." We assume our future will look like our present. That quiet optimism makes planning feel optional.
- We confuse simple with safe. People say, "I don't have much," or "My family gets along." The problem is that big estate-planning messes can, and often do, show up in everyday families because

there are assets involved that still trigger legal and financial consequences when no one has authority to act.

- We underestimate the life part of estate planning. Many people think estate planning is only about death. In reality, the most urgent problems, like a sudden hospitalization, a stroke, an accident, or a cognitive decline, show up during life. That's when families discover they can't access accounts, talk to providers, or make decisions without the right documents.
- We don't want to open the emotional door. Talking about incapacity and death can feel like inviting it in. Add complicated family dynamics—second marriages, strained siblings, unequal gifts, old resentments—and it becomes even easier to say, "We'll deal with it later."
- We're waiting for the right time that never comes. People put estate planning on the mental shelf with other important, but not urgent tasks: update the beneficiaries, organize the records, write the will. The shelf gets crowded. The months pass. And eventually, something happens—and the people you love are left to navigate decisions you could have made calmly, in advance.

Estate planning is how you guide your loved ones through a minefield they don't even realize they'll have to cross—until they're already in it.

If any of these reasons feel familiar, you're in the right place. The goal of this book isn't to guilt you into action. It's to make the process clearer, lighter, and more doable—so you can move forward with confidence instead of postponing it indefinitely.

> Estate planning is how you guide your loved ones through a minefield they don't even realize they'll have to cross—until they're already in it.

Personal Story

For me, estate planning isn't just professional, it's personal. I lost my mother in a car crash when I was young, and it permanently changed the way I think about what families need when life turns upside down.

When the news came, the adults in my family were blindsided. As a teenager, I watched people I trusted struggle to answer questions none of us expected to face: Who makes decisions now? What would she have wanted? What happens next? The shock was immediate, but what lingered was the uncertainty—because my mother was young and didn't have an estate plan.

She was a nurse. To me, she was a superhero—someone who spent her life caring for other people. Like so many working parents, she put everyone else first. Planning for herself, her wishes, and her what-if scenarios felt unnecessary.

After she died, my family wanted to do right by her. We wanted to honor her. But we didn't have written guidance, and we hadn't had the kind of conversations that would have helped us fill in the gaps. We were left guessing about things that felt deeply personal: how she would have wanted her children cared for, what she would have wanted for her remains, and how she would have wanted her hard-earned assets handled. We did our best. But grief makes even "simple" decisions heavy—and it can turn uncertainty into conflict.

That experience taught me something I've seen repeated in my practice again and again: Estate planning isn't about the paperwork. It's about clarity and guidance.

You don't have to see the whole staircase,
just take the first step.
—Martin Luther King, Jr.

The Role Of Clarity And Communication

One of the most powerful benefits of estate planning is that it reduces guesswork.

When your intentions are written down and legally supported, your loved ones don't have to argue over your wishes. They don't have to ask, "What would she have wanted?" while they're exhausted, grieving, and under pressure from hospitals, banks, and sometimes other family members. They can follow a plan you created when you were calm, clearheaded, and able to think things through.

That clarity doesn't just prevent delays—it can prevent conflict. Many family disputes related to inheritance are fueled by uncertainty and a lack of communication. Silence creates a vacuum, and into that vacuum, people fill in the blanks with assumptions, old habits, family dynamics, and worst-case interpretations.

Communication is the safety valve.

You don't have to share every detail or every dollar amount of your estate plan. But telling the right people the basics—where the documents are, who is in charge, and what you want your plan to accomplish—can make the difference between a smooth administration and a painful mess.

Estate planning isn't just a set of legal documents. It's also a set of instructions. The documents provide authority. The instructions provide context.

> Communication is the safety valve.

What Comes Next

If you're feeling unsure where to start, you're not alone. One of the biggest reasons people avoid estate planning is that it feels overwhelming—too many options, too many "what-ifs," and too much pressure to get it perfect.

I wrote this book to help make it more manageable.

In the chapters ahead, we'll break down the major tools of an estate plan—what they do, what they don't do, and how they work together. You'll learn how planning protects you during life (especially during incapacity), how it protects your loved ones after death, and where people unintentionally create problems even when they have documents in place.

You'll also see why estate planning isn't a finish-it-and-forget-it proposition. It should evolve and be updated as your life, relationships, and finances change. It is a framework that should match your real life—your relationships, your assets, your values, and the people you trust to carry things out. It should not be something that only worked for you years ago.

My goal isn't to overwhelm you or scare you into action. It's to give you clarity and confidence—so you can move forward deliberately, avoid common traps, and build a plan that actually works when it matters.

Because the best time to plan is before the emergency.

Key Takeaways

Estate planning is about life, not just death.
It's the act of documenting your wishes so you and your loved ones are protected—whether you're healthy, ill, or gone.

Doing nothing is still a decision.
When you don't plan, your state's law decides who handles your affairs, who cares for your children, and who inherits your property.

Clarity prevents conflict.
Putting your wishes in writing reduces confusion, stress, and disagreements among family members.

Planning is an act of love.
It's not about paperwork—it's about care, responsibility, and easing the weight on those left behind.

Chapter 3

Scams And Elder Financial Abuse

The Shocking Truth

Chance favors only the prepared mind.
—Louis Pasteur

Estate planning isn't only about where your money goes after you're gone—it's also about protecting it while you're still here. One of the most overlooked risks in today's world is financial exploitation, especially among older adults.

Before I began helping families with estate planning, I served as a prosecutor, handling financial crime and elder abuse cases. I saw firsthand how quickly trust can be manipulated and how easily victims lose everything. Now, as an estate planning attorney, I meet families who never imagined it could happen to them—until it did.

It's easy to think of estate planning as something that sits quietly in the background, waiting for someday when we get around to actually doing it. But some families and individuals who never get around to planning may regret it because a serious fraud or theft can drain their savings and estate before they realize it. I'm talking about scams, financial exploitation, and elder financial abuse, which have all become alarmingly common in recent years.

Fraud rarely begins with a stranger in the shadows. More often, it starts with a familiar voice: a family member, caregiver, or new "friend" who gradually earns access and influence. By the time the deception is recognized, the damage—financial, emotional, and often legal—can be devastating.

I prosecuted a variety of cases, including elaborate financial scams and cases of elder abuse. I saw firsthand how quickly a lifetime's worth of savings could be wiped out, and how trusting people become unwitting targets. As we age, the risks of illness such as dementia, Alzheimer's disease, or other health challenges can make even the most capable people vulnerable.

The truth is that financial exploitation can affect anyone. Without the right safeguards, we risk not only our savings but the legacy we've worked so hard to build.

That's why estate planning and fraud prevention go hand in hand. A well-designed plan doesn't just pass wealth forward—it shields it from those who might try to take it unfairly.

> The truth is that financial exploitation can affect anyone. Without the right safeguards, we risk not only our savings but the legacy we've worked so hard to build.

The Growing Threat

I don't write this to be alarmist or scare people into planning, but I do want to raise awareness of the realities of this issue. Financial exploitation of older adults has reached crisis levels in the United States. According to the National Council on Aging, older Americans lose an estimated $28 billion each year to scams, theft, and financial abuse.[5] And experts believe that number represents only a fraction of actual cases, since most go unreported—often out of shame or fear.[6]

While scams can happen to anyone, older adults are often targeted because they may have more saved, be isolated from family members, or be dealing with declining health.

Technology has made fraud easier and more convincing. Scammers impersonate government agencies, banks, and even family members. They use emotional pressure—urgency, fear, or affection—to manipulate decisions. But while digital scams make headlines, most elder exploitation still happens the old-fashioned way: through misplaced trust.

A widowed parent might rely on a neighbor or caregiver who slowly takes over financial responsibilities. A well-meaning adult child might commingle funds, rationalizing that "Mom would have wanted this anyway." Even unscrupulous professionals—financial advisors, contractors, or business partners—can exploit a position of trust when proper checks aren't in place.

Even if you feel confident in your ability to spot a scam, it's worth knowing that scammers are becoming more sophisticated every year. Phone calls that appear to come from the Internal Revenue Service (IRS), emails that look like they're from your bank or law enforcement, or urgent messages about a grandchild in trouble—these tricks are designed to create panic and get people to act fast.

The effects are often irreversible. Victims lose life savings, and families fracture under the weight of the blame and betrayal.

The Emotional Toll

Beyond the obvious financial damage, I've seen how scams and financial abuse unravel families and leave lasting scars. Victims often struggle with guilt, embarrassment, or denial. In some cases, the abuser is someone close: a caregiver, a relative, or even a trusted friend. These betrayals are particularly painful because they're not just about lost money, they're about lost trust.

If you've ever witnessed the aftermath of a scam, you know the effects can linger for years. I've met people who still blame themselves for falling for it, or families who now second-guess every decision because of what happened to a loved one. Sometimes people blame themselves for not being more involved in their elderly loved one's care, believing they might have been able to stop the scam. I occasionally get calls from concerned family members worried about the everyday risks their aging family members face. They ask me for advice on protecting the vulnerable adult from the onslaught of scams targeting them.

The afternoon knows what the morning never suspected.

—Robert Frost

Building A First Line Of Defense

Awareness is the strongest early defense against exploitation. The earlier you identify risks, the more options you have to stop them.

Start by staying connected. Isolation is one of the biggest predictors of financial abuse. Regular contact with trusted friends, family members, or advisors can create natural checks and balances. Encourage open discussions about finances, upcoming medical procedures, and changes in daily routines. When information flows freely, it's harder for manipulation to take root. If you have a reliable financial advisor, they can provide support if something seems suspicious—like a sudden change in your spending, or a new friend, roommate, or caretaker showing up and pressuring you to move your money.

Banks and investment firms now allow you to designate a trusted contact person who can be alerted if suspicious activity occurs and you cannot be reached. This isn't a joint owner or power of attorney agent; it's simply a safety contact. Many families overlook this simple step, yet it can be the first signal that something's wrong before major losses occur. This doesn't mean you need to give them immediate control over your finances, but it does mean making sure you have reliable people listed on your accounts and in your estate plan.

Technology can also help. Online account alerts, spending notifications, and two-factor authentication all add layers of security that are worth considering. But tools are only as effective as the communication behind them. If you have adult children or close friends who help with your finances, make sure they know what your normal activity looks like—and when to ask questions.

Most importantly, don't dismiss your instincts. If something feels off, it probably is. Fraudsters often count on tricking people into a scam by acting without careful consideration. They try to create fear or urgency.

This is where asking questions, seeking a second opinion, or calling a professional advisor can interrupt the pattern before harm occurs.

How Can Estate Planning Protect You?

A thorough estate plan does more than decide who gets what. A well-designed plan creates legal guardrails that make financial exploitation much harder for those who do not have your best interests at heart. Here's how.

Financial Power Of Attorney

Designating a trusted financial agent allows someone you choose—not a stranger or a court—to act if you can't. You control when that authority begins and ends, and you can limit it to specific actions. This is a serious responsibility, and you should assign it to someone you think might be up for the task.

Medical Power Of Attorney And Advance Directives

These documents appoint someone to make healthcare decisions if you become unable to. Without them, family members may have to go to court for permission to act, creating stress and delay when time matters most.

Revocable Living Trust

For many families, a living trust adds another layer of protection. By naming a responsible trustee and successor trustee, you control who manages your assets when you're alive and can't do it yourself, and after you pass away. This structure can reduce court involvement and allow for continuous management if illness or incapacity strikes.

Professional Oversight And Dual Controls

If no trustworthy family member is available, consider appointing a vetted professional fiduciary or trust company. You can also consider requiring dual signatures as a safeguard against potential abuse.

Together, these tools form a security system around your finances and personal care. They don't just protect your assets; they protect your independence, dignity, and peace of mind.

Practical Tips To Spot And Avoid Scams

Even the most cautious people can be deceived. Scams rely on playing with human emotion and psychology. Fear, urgency, curiosity, and compassion are the levers that make even the most rational person hesitate for just long enough to be manipulated.

Financial exploitation comes in many forms, but many of them share three common traits: urgency, secrecy, and pressure. The details vary, but the playbook is similar.

The "Fear And Urgency" Scam

How would you react if you received a call claiming your Social Security number has been suspended, you're delinquent in paying a fine, your bank account is frozen, or a loved one is in jail?[7] The voice sounds official—sometimes even friendly—and insists you must act immediately. They may demand payment, personal information, or gift cards as verification.

Red flag: Real agencies never demand immediate payment or ask for confidential details over the phone. The IRS will never call you; official communications are done by mail.[8] Hang up and call the agency directly using the number on an official statement or website.

> Financial exploitation comes in many forms, but many of them share three common traits: urgency, secrecy, and pressure.

The "Romance Or Caregiver" Scam

Loneliness is a growing epidemic, especially among older adults. Scammers exploit emotional vulnerability by pretending to form relationships online or through caregiving roles. Over time, they ask for help with emergencies, unexpected expenses, or investments.

Red flag: Anyone who builds rapid emotional intimacy and ties it to money should raise your suspicion. Discuss new relationships with trusted friends, family members, or advisors before sending funds or sharing information.

The "Family Or Friend In Need" Scam

Fraudsters sometimes impersonate a grandchild, niece, or friend using stolen information from social media. They claim to need bail money, emergency medical funds, or help while traveling abroad. Don't fall for it and independently verify information when possible.

Red flag: Urgency combined with secrecy, "Don't tell Mom or Dad," is a telltale sign since calling Mom or Dad would be most people's first resort. Pause and verify before reacting emotionally.

The "Investment Or Sweepstakes" Scam

Too-good-to-be-true investment offers or you've-won-a-prize messages are among the oldest scams. They promise guaranteed profits, lottery winnings, or incredible investment opportunities—but always with a catch. Many victims are asked to pay small processing or tax fees before receiving their supposed payout. That is where they trick people into paying them in exchange for nothing.

These scams don't just target the elderly or financially inexperienced. I once reviewed a case involving a person who fell for what she believed was a legitimate sweepstakes. When she couldn't afford to pay the tax on her supposed winnings, the scammers offered her an alternative. They asked for her help to clear and cash checks for other winners through her personal bank account. The checks were actually the tax payments that other victims made in hopes of receiving prizes.

She became an unwitting accomplice. She deposited the victims' checks, withdrew the cash, and mailed it to the scammers. By the time the truth surfaced, she was facing multiple felony charges in several states. The scam had been part of a nationwide fraud ring.

This case highlights the fact that victims are often trusting, helpful, and simply unaware of how sophisticated these schemes have become.

Red flag: Any winning that requires you to pay fees, transfer money for others, or handle checks on someone else's behalf is a scam. No legitimate sweepstakes or investment will ever ask for advance payment to receive your prize or return.

The Psychology Behind Many Scams

Most schemes—no matter how sophisticated—rely on emotion over logic. Scammers know that stress, confusion, or excitement can overcome our good judgment. That's why they push urgency. Scammers don't want you to stop and think about it.

Recognizing this emotional manipulation is your strongest defense. If you feel pressured, confused, or uneasy, *pause*. Talk to someone you trust or call your financial institution before acting. A five-minute conversation can save you lots of regret later.

Communication and keeping trusted family and friends informed also help to reduce the prevalence of scams. Check in regularly with your trusted contacts and encourage your family members to do the same. Open communication is one of the best safeguards. If something doesn't feel right, ask a known professional or someone you trust for advice before taking action.

A Case That Still Haunts Me

I remember many of the really disturbing cases from my time as a prosecutor, but this one still haunts me.

An older woman, let's call her Agatha—sharp, independent, and deeply trusting—began relying on a distant relative to help manage her daily errands after a minor surgery. At first, he seemed generous. He helped Agatha with grocery shopping, picking up prescriptions, and paying bills online. But within a few months, it turned out that Agatha's accounts were drained of thousands of dollars.

When the theft was discovered, the damage wasn't only financial. The betrayal devastated her confidence. Agatha felt ashamed for letting it happen and leaving her guard down. Her caring family members turned inward, arguing over who should have noticed sooner and checked on Mom more often. By the time the case reached my desk, Agatha's physical health had declined, and so had her independence.

Legally, we were able to hold the perpetrator accountable—but no amount of legal restitution restored what she'd lost emotionally. What could have made the difference? Adding a trusted family member or friend as a trusted contact or power of attorney agent on her accounts with visibility into what was happening. Agatha could have chosen who would help her handle her finances and under what terms. Instead, the perpetrator isolated Agatha from other family members and took away her credit and debit cards while using them himself.

I think of her often when I meet families in my practice today. It's rarely a matter of carelessness; many people simply never imagined they could become targets. Yet the truth is that none of us is immune to manipulation, especially in moments of vulnerability.

That case taught me that planning ahead isn't just about protecting money; it's about protecting dignity, confidence, and the right to choose who stands beside you when life becomes uncertain.

Awareness Is The First Step

The reality of scams and exploitation can be unsettling, but fear isn't the goal—preparation is.

The same planning tools that protect your legacy can also help protect you from exploitation.

A clear estate plan builds a circle of trust and transparency that makes it harder for a scammer to steal from you. Talking openly with loved ones, naming responsible agents, and reviewing your plan every few years are small steps that create lasting protection.

Awareness is where it starts. Action is what secures it.

In the next chapter, we'll look at another silent risk—what happens when no plan exists at all—and how easily control can slip away when decisions are left to the courts.

Key Takeaways

Financial exploitation is widespread.
Older Americans lose billions each year to scams, most of which go unreported.

The most common scams follow familiar patterns.
According to the FBI[9] and FTC,[10] the leading schemes include tech support, romance, "grandparent," government impersonation, and sweepstakes scams.

Legal planning builds strong defenses.
Financial and medical powers of attorney, living trusts, and clear fiduciary oversight create accountability and deter abuse.

Connection prevents isolation.
Open communication with family, friends, and professionals makes it harder to hide manipulation.

Chapter 4

The Silent Threat
What Happens When You Don't Plan

Dig the well before you are thirsty.
—Chinese Proverb

Many people think of estate planning as something only the wealthy or the elderly need to address later in life. But one of the most profound misunderstandings is that it's only a problem after you die. I have heard people say, "I'll be dead, so I won't care what happens." The truth is that the bigger risk often arrives while you're still alive, but can't speak for yourself. I'm talking about incapacity. Emergencies. Sudden illness. When there's no plan in place, the lack of planning can quickly turn into a crisis, even with trustworthy people around us.

Good Intentions Aren't Enough

I've talked to many people who assumed everything would simply work out—that love, trust, and common sense would be enough if something went wrong. They believed the right person could step in automatically, or that their modest assets didn't justify formal planning.

But legal administration of someone's estate doesn't run on good intentions or "everyone knows what I would want."

It runs on written legal authority, documentation, and procedure. Without that structure and guidance in place, families can quickly find themselves pulled into court processes that are confusing, expensive, and emotionally draining.

> Legal administration of someone's estate doesn't run on good intentions or "everyone knows what I would want."

When No One Has Legal Authority

Let's talk about what happens when there is no plan. If you lose the ability to manage your affairs—due to a stroke, cognitive decline, an accident, or any number of reasons—your loved ones can't simply start making decisions for you. Financial institutions and medical providers require legal authorization before they can take direction from your loved ones.

Financially speaking, this becomes a real mess if you have lots of individual accounts, retirement accounts that need to be accessed, or separate credit cards. Without a durable power of attorney in place, your family may need to get a court involved to get decision-making authority through a process called guardianship or conservatorship.

Medical Decisions And The HIPAA Wall

On the medical side, things can also get complicated very quickly. If you haven't named someone to make healthcare decisions for you, no one has that authority, even your spouse or adult children. Hospitals and doctors will not guess who should be in charge, and they aren't allowed to take direction from someone just because they're next of kin. It doesn't work the same way as parents making decisions for their young children.

State law governs how someone is elevated to the position of making medical decisions for you if you did not specify your preference in writing. Sometimes this means having someone petition a court to be appointed as a person's guardian. In other instances, a healthcare proxy may be selected by family members, only if they all agree on who that person should be. This isn't a good situation to put family members through, especially if it could lead to family disagreements.

To top things off, we have to add confidential patient information into the mix.

Without a signed HIPAA release or healthcare power of attorney, your loved ones may not be able to get updates about your condition, much less make critical decisions on your behalf. I've spoken with families frozen out of hospital rooms, unable to access medical records, or forced to go to court just to get permission to speak with a care team. In those moments, fear and helplessness take over, not because families don't care, but because they're legally powerless to help.

Don't assume these scenarios are rare. A car accident. A sudden stroke. A serious fall. These are some real-life triggers that show just how fragile our assumption that "my loved ones will take care of me" really is. Without a clear legal plan in place, the consequences can snowball into confusion, panic, and delay. These scenarios are when clarity and promptness are exactly what's needed.

The guardianship court process isn't quick or easy. It involves filing legal paperwork, paying fees, and attending hearings. A judge evaluates the filings in front of them, appoints a guardian, and imposes ongoing court oversight. Your life—and your money—become part of the public record. Worse, if there's disagreement among your family members about who should serve, the court battle can turn ugly fast.

According to national surveys, 58 percent of adults in the US say they or someone they know has experienced family conflict due to the absence of an estate plan or will.[11]

Conflict doesn't always come from greed—often, it starts with confusion, surprise, and emotional stress.

In my own practice, I've seen siblings stop speaking with each other for years after arguing over who should manage a parent's finances or care. Sometimes those arguments begin with love—a shared concern for a parent's wellbeing—but without a clear legal structure, trust unravels quickly.

> Conflict doesn't always come from greed—often, it starts with confusion, surprise, and emotional stress.

When Families Disagree

One family I helped faced exactly that situation. The father, a retired school principal, never got around to creating a power of attorney. After a medical crisis left him unconscious, his two children disagreed on nearly every decision. The son wanted to move him into a care facility. The daughter insisted he return home with in-home support. Each believed they were doing the right thing. But without written authority, neither could act. The court eventually appointed a professional guardian—a stranger—to take over. The financial cost was high; the emotional cost was higher.

This kind of court involvement isn't rare. In fact, more than two-thirds of Americans likely lack a documented incapacity plan—meaning the majority of families are at risk of falling into a similar situation.[12] It doesn't just affect the elderly. Accidents and illnesses don't wait for retirement.

The consequences of not planning extend beyond incapacity. Dying without a will or trust means your estate could be distributed under state "intestacy" laws—a one-size-fits-all formula that rarely matches your wishes. These intestacy laws don't consider unmarried partners, charities, friends, stepchildren, or your personal wishes.

The Hidden Cost Of Court Involvement

Probate, the court process for settling an estate, adds more complications. Guardianship and probate processes are neither quick nor cheap. Filing fees, attorney costs, and ongoing reporting expenses add up fast. On top of that, every detail of your finances and personal affairs becomes public. Probate fees typically consume between 3 percent and 7 percent of an estate's value.[13] That means a $400,000 estate could lose as much as $28,000 just in court and attorney fees!

Planning isn't just about creating legal documents; it's also important to keep our loved ones in the loop. Even when people do plan, their loved ones often don't know where the documents are—or that they've even been named in a role of responsibility in a loved one's document. According to recent data, 52 percent of people don't even know where their parents' estate documents are stored.[14] Even more concerning, only 46 percent of people named as personal representatives in someone's will are aware they've been named.[15] This information gap slows everything down and piles stress on top of grief.

Planning ahead solves most of these problems. Not all at once, and not perfectly—but planning proactively puts you in charge. When you document your wishes and talk to the people involved, you eliminate guesswork. You create clarity. You reduce conflict. You stay in control of your life and legacy, even when you can't speak for yourself.

A plan doesn't have to be perfect—it just has to exist. Even a few essential documents can mean the difference between chaos and clarity. Estate planning doesn't have to be expensive or intimidating. The hardest part, often, is getting started. In the next chapter, we'll explore the most common reason people delay planning: procrastination—and how to move past it before life makes the decision for us.

Key Takeaways

Incapacity can strike anyone.
Estate planning isn't only about passing your stuff to your loved ones—it's about maintaining control while you're still alive.

Without documents, families can't act.
Courts decide who manages finances and medical care when no financial power of attorney or healthcare power of attorney exist.

Court intervention is costly and public.
Guardianship and probate proceedings drain time, privacy, and resources.

Intestacy laws rarely reflect personal wishes.
Without a will or trust, state formulas determine inheritance.

Communication matters as much as documentation.
Planning ahead and sharing key details prevent confusion, conflict, and delay.

Chapter 5

The Procrastination Trap

"I'll Get To It Later"

Fix the roof while the sun is shining.

—John F. Kennedy

Procrastination is the quiet killer of good intentions. We all do it. We put things off because they're uncomfortable, unfamiliar, frustrating, or feel too far away to matter today. And estate planning? It's the perfect candidate for delay. It touches on money, mortality, family dynamics, and legal complexity—all things most people would rather not deal with when life is already busy.

But "I'll get to it later" often becomes "I never got around to it." We just refuse to believe that something catastrophic could happen to us.

Psychologists call this the optimism bias—the tendency to believe that bad things happen to other people, not to us.[16] It's why we assume the accident, the illness, or the unexpected crisis can strike someone else's family, but not our own. This feeling of confidence helps us stay positive, but it also lulls us into a false sense of security, leaving us unprepared. When it comes to estate planning, optimism bias whispers that there's still time—that the "someday" we've been promising ourselves will arrive before anything goes wrong.

Many people I work with are so relieved after completing their estate plans, but proper timing is always important. People have told me they postponed their estate planning for years because the conversation felt too heavy. When a sudden illness hit, they scrambled to finalize documents between hospital visits. They told me afterward they wished they'd treated estate planning like insurance, something you take care of before you need it.

In my conversations with clients, I have learned that procrastination is a common reason they delay creating a plan. And it's not just anecdotal. National data backs this up: 43 percent of people who haven't created a will say it's because they just haven't gotten around to it.[17] Even among high-income earners—those making over $80,000 a year—the number jumps to 63 percent.[18] These are people who have assets to protect and recognize the importance of planning, yet the plan still doesn't get done. I have even met plenty of attorneys who still haven't done their own wills or estate planning despite recognizing the need.

But people of all walks of life tend to put off this important planning. They say the same things: "Someday I'll get around to it." An even more staggering statistic: 37 percent of people say a serious illness would motivate them to get a will.[19] Do we really need something bad to happen before we take action? Absolutely not.

So Why Do We Wait?

The reasons are relatable. Life moves fast. We prioritize the urgent over the important. Planning for what might happen someday gets pushed aside by what's happening right now. Some people avoid estate planning because it forces them to confront uncomfortable questions: What if I get sick? What happens to my kids? Who should I trust with my decisions? These aren't easy questions. But not asking them doesn't make the risks go away.

The irony is that procrastinating on planning doesn't actually make life easier. It creates vulnerability and sometimes anxiety for putting it off. And if something unexpected happens—a medical emergency, an accident, a death—the cost of delay isn't just measured in dollars. It's measured in confusion, court intervention, family stress, and the burden passed on to people you care about.

I lost count of the clients who waited until a diagnosis forced the issue; they reached out to me in panic, and we were racing against the clock to complete the estate plan in a time crunch. I often hear things like, "We should have done this long ago, but we never got around to it." As they belatedly ask for help, the pressure is high. Emotions are raw. With other looming things on their mind, they have to make many intricate decisions. And those decisions are now being rushed.

There's a dangerous myth embedded in procrastination: that doing nothing is neutral.

It's not. Doing nothing is making a conscious decision, not the one you would have made if you got a do-over. If you don't put a plan in place, you are choosing to accept the default plan that your state imposes on all the people without a plan. Intestacy laws, court-appointed guardianships and conservatorships, and contested probate proceedings are the legal realities many families face when there is no plan in place. That's what's behind the curtain when we leave things for later.

> There's a dangerous myth embedded in procrastination: that doing nothing is neutral.

The Illusion Of Time

Let's consider Brian as an example. He came to me after his partner's sudden hospitalization for a terminal illness. They had talked about getting a plan in place after the holidays, but they never made it that far. Brian's partner was now unconscious, but Brian wasn't legally recognized as next of kin. He couldn't access his partner's accounts. He couldn't speak for his partner medically. He couldn't even enter his partner's apartment without legal permission. All of it could have been avoided—with one meeting, a few signed documents, and an honest conversation they never got around to. I understand this does not happen in every case, but feeling like you are out of options and without a way out of the legal maze when it is too late to plan can be very devastating.

Optimism bias isn't the only force at work. Some barriers come not from what we believe about the future, but from what we fear in the present.

There's nothing fun about stuff like estate planning, getting mammograms, or talking to a guy about long-term disability insurance, but you do it anyway. Trust me, the stress of not having done the above is prematurely aging.

—Jen Lancaster

Fear, Discomfort, And The "Someday" Trap

Even when we know planning is important, something deeper often stops us. It isn't laziness, it's discomfort. Estate planning forces us to face topics that feel personal, uncertain, and final. Thinking about mortality or imagining illness makes most people instinctively pull away. So, we tell ourselves we'll handle it *someday*.

But "someday" is a clever illusion. It's comfortable because we don't have to commit—close enough to keep us feeling we are in control and responsible, but distant enough to avoid action now. It lets us believe we're still in control, even while doing nothing. In psychology, this is known as avoidance behavior—the tendency to sidestep tasks that stir anxiety or sadness.[20] We aren't avoiding the plan; we're avoiding the feelings that come with it.

For some people, the fear centers on making a mistake—naming the wrong person, misunderstanding the legal process, or missing a detail that could cause problems later. For others, it's about conflict—worrying how family members will react to being included or excluded, or whether conversations about money will reopen old wounds. A surprising number of clients admit that they've delayed planning because they didn't want to "jinx" their good health, as if writing things down might somehow invite tragedy.

The truth is that fear and discomfort are natural responses to uncertainty. The challenge isn't to erase them, it's to work *through* them. Planning isn't about predicting every possibility; it's about reducing chaos for the people who will one day need to step in.

I once worked with a woman who said she had a mental block about estate planning. She was young, healthy, and busy raising two children. She didn't want to think about what might happen "if." When a medical emergency landed her husband in the hospital, she realized how quickly life can flip from predictable to precarious. Within a week, she completed her entire plan—not because her fear vanished, but because she understood that planning wasn't about expecting the worst. It was about protecting peace of mind and her kids.

The first step doesn't have to be perfect—it just has to be taken.

Call one professional. Have one conversation. Sign one document. Each small action chips away at uncertainty and builds a sense of control.

The "someday" trap can disappear the moment you take that first real step toward protecting what matters most.

Even a basic plan is often better than no plan at all. You can revise it as you go. In fact, you should revise it as you go because the plan should evolve with you and fit your current circumstances. Life changes. Plans evolve. But you can't improve what doesn't exist, so getting started somewhere is important.

That's where it begins. And beginning the plan gives you momentum to get it done.

> The first step doesn't have to be perfect—
> it just has to be taken.

Simple Steps To Start

We often treat planning as an obligation, but it is really a gift to our future selves and to those we love.

The hardest part is simply beginning. Once you take the first step, the process feels less like a burden and more like peace of mind made visible.

If you're reading this and feeling behind, you're not alone. But the worst thing you can do is let that feeling keep you frozen. Start where you are. Take one step. Make one call. Write down your wishes. Talk to someone you trust. Schedule the appointment you've been meaning to make and have been putting off. Organize your accounts and review your beneficiaries.

Procrastination is normal. But regret is optional.

Understanding why we wait is half the battle. The next step is to challenge the biggest myth of all—the idea that we simply don't need a plan yet.

> We often treat planning as an obligation, but it is really a gift to our future selves and to those we love.

Key Takeaways

Procrastination is normal, but we should be aware of it.
Understanding why we delay is the first step toward acting.

Optimism bias keeps us waiting.
We believe bad outcomes happen to others—until experience proves otherwise.

Time feels infinite—until it isn't.
The right time rarely announces itself. Starting small breaks the cycle of delay.

Conversations create momentum.
Talking about planning turns intention into action and removes fear's power.

Planning is self-care disguised as paperwork.
It's how we protect peace of mind—for ourselves and those we love.

Chapter 6

The "It Won't Happen To Me" Myth

He who has no plan will be defeated in every battle.
—Arabic proverb

Once we understand why we delay, the next question becomes how we justify it and keep putting it off. A quiet voice in the back of many people's minds speaks up when the thought of estate planning comes up. It says: "I'm healthy. I'm young. I'm not rich. Nothing drastic is going to happen to me anytime soon." If we convince ourselves that any of these things is true, we tend to think estate planning is not for us.

That voice giving us justifications for not planning is the reason so many people don't plan. But that voice is wrong. Planning when you are healthy, building up assets, and have plenty of time to make difficult decisions is the best way to do it.

One of the most dangerous myths about estate planning is that it's only necessary for the elderly, the wealthy, or the seriously ill. But nearly every week, I work with families that tell me everything was fine until their lives were turned upside down by something unexpected. Accidents don't check your bank account before they happen. Illnesses don't care how old you are. And we don't get a warning before becoming incapacitated due to a serious injury or illness.

Reality Check

Statistically, people who've experienced serious illness in their families are 66 percent more likely to create an estate plan.[21] Why? Because once you've lived through it, the rose-colored glasses come off. You see firsthand how hard it is to navigate uncertainty without guidance; we don't want to repeat the mistakes of our loved ones who had no plan in place. You feel how heavy it is to guess at someone's wishes, or to make decisions when nothing's written down. You learn—sometimes too late—that not having a plan doesn't just create confusion. It creates conflict.

None of this is about being pessimistic. It's about being prepared.

The people who take the time to create a plan aren't being morbid. They're being thoughtful.

They're making the effort to plan—not because they expect the worst to happen, but because they want the peace of mind that comes from knowing they've done everything they can to help if the worst does happen.

I've had countless conversations that start the same way: "I never thought we'd be in this situation." And then the next sentence: "I wish we had done this sooner."

Let's explore the common myths I hear too often.

> The people who take the time to create a plan aren't being morbid. They're being thoughtful.

"I Don't Have Enough Money To Need A Plan"—The Modest-Means Bias

Many people assume estate planning is for the wealthy—those with complex assets, multiple homes, private yachts, or large investment portfolios. But every estate, regardless of size, still needs direction. Contrary to popular belief, there is no minimum amount needed before you have earned the "luxury" of an estate plan.

Even simple assets—a checking account, a car, a home, or life insurance—can trigger legal procedures if ownership or beneficiaries aren't clear. Still, the belief persists. One in three Americans without a will say they don't have one because they don't think they have enough money or assets to justify it.[22] Forty percent believe they're "too poor" for estate planning to matter.[23] But these beliefs completely miss the point. Estate planning is not about the size of your bank account. It's about control, clarity, and care—for yourself and the people who rely on you.

Consider unmarried couples. If one partner ends up in the hospital without naming the other in legal documents, they may have no right to access medical information or make decisions—no matter how long they've lived together or how committed they are. The law doesn't recognize feelings. It recognizes legal documents.

Same-sex couples, even those who are married, have historically faced enormous legal hurdles when plans weren't in place. And while marriage equality has addressed many of the legal gaps, it hasn't changed the need for formal planning—especially around inheritance, medical authority, and end-of-life decisions. Planning is how you protect the life you've built.

For parents, the stakes are even higher. Without estate planning, there's no way to legally nominate a guardian who you want to raise your minor children if something happens to you. Without your input, that decision is left completely up to the courts. Although the court system is typically designed to find a solution in the best interest of children, these types of cases can and often do take lots of time, invite disputes, and end up naming someone you may have never chosen yourself. It's one of the most important reasons to plan, and yet surveys show that Americans with children under eighteen are among the least likely to have an estate plan.[24] That statistic should keep us all up at night.

Only put off until tomorrow
what you are willing to die having left undone.
—Pablo Picasso

"I'm Too Young For That"—The Young And Healthy Bias

It's easy to believe that estate planning is something for *later*—after retirement, after the mortgage is paid, after the kids are grown. When you're healthy and busy, the future feels predictable. But health and young age don't protect us from accidents or sudden illness.

I met a couple in their thirties who postponed creating even basic powers of attorney. They were active, healthy, and building their careers. Then an unexpected car accident left one of them in a medically induced coma for weeks. The healthy spouse couldn't access the other spouse's accounts or insurance paperwork because they kept separate accounts. Their story is far from rare.

And then there are the young adults, especially those just heading off to college or entering the workforce. Once a child turns eighteen, their parents can no longer legally make medical or financial decisions on their behalf. I've seen the panic on a parent's face when their twenty-year-old ends up in the ER after an accident, and they realize they can't even speak with the doctors. A healthcare power of attorney could have made all the difference. We will discuss healthcare powers of attorney in detail in chapter 13.

"My Family Will Figure It Out"— The Oversimplification Assumption

Many people truly believe their situation is too simple to need formal planning.

They'll say, "Everything's joint," or "My kids get along," or "We don't have much to divide." It feels comforting to think that love and common sense will smooth everything over. But when no plan exists, and the family is dealing with stress and grief from the loss of a loved one or a major medical event, even straightforward lives can become complicated in a hurry.

Even the simplest situations and estates need structure.

Clarity prevents conflict before it starts. Planning doesn't replace trust—it reinforces it by giving your loved ones a clear road map when they need it most.

The idea that "My family will figure it out" underestimates both the complexity of the legal system and the emotional weight of loss. In grief, even small decisions—such as who signs forms, who pays bills, and who manages accounts—can become enormous. A written plan turns uncertainty into guidance, protecting relationships from the pressure of guesswork.

> Even the simplest situations and estates need structure.

Reframing The Mindset

All these myths stem from the same place—good intentions and the belief that there's still time. But time has a way of slipping through our fingers. The next section explores what happens when later finally arrives and the plan still doesn't exist.

Estate planning often carries a heavy emotional label. People associate it with aging, loss, or illness. But the truth is that planning is less about endings and more about *readiness.*

Creating a will or trust doesn't mean you expect the worst—it means you're prepared in case something does happen. A good plan gives you confidence to make decisions now and flexibility to adjust later. It grows with you as your life changes.

I often joke with clients and tell them my best advice is "don't die or let your health decline." But if you don't take my best advice, you still have a backup: your estate plan. You hope you won't need it soon, but you're grateful that it's there when life throws you a surprise. The plan isn't about replacing something you lost; it's about protecting what you still have—time, options, and peace of mind.

Estate planning helps prevent the regret of "I wish we took care of this sooner." It's how you keep the unnecessary weight off their shoulders. It's how you make hard times just a little bit easier.

In the next chapter, we'll talk about what to do when it all feels overwhelming—how to break down the process into manageable steps, and why you don't have to figure everything out at once to get started.

Key Takeaways

The phrase "I don't need a plan yet" is the most expensive myth in estate planning.
Waiting feels harmless, but you give up your wishes and control to the courts.

Health and age don't guarantee readiness.
Emergencies and incapacity can happen at any stage of life, regardless of income, health, or best intentions.

Estate planning isn't about wealth; it's about direction.
Even modest estates need clear instructions for who acts, who decides, and who inherits.

Trust alone isn't a plan.
We should not rely on our families to figure it out without written guidance; clarity preserves relationships when emotions run high.

Planning early is an act of readiness, not fear.
Starting now brings immediate peace of mind and ensures your wishes—not assumptions—guide the future.

Chapter 7

Overwhelmed And Confused?

How To Make Sense Of It All

Failing to plan is planning to fail.
—Anonymous

It's completely normal to feel overwhelmed by estate planning. The words alone—probate, power of attorney, fiduciary, intestacy, healthcare directive, living will—sound like a foreign language. Then, we add to the confusion: our emotions, family dynamics, financial worries, and the fact that none of us can predict the future. It's easy to see why so many people freeze.

I've seen it firsthand: Intelligent, responsible adults who've handled everything else in their lives with confidence are suddenly unsure of how to start this process and don't know who might be the best fit to be the guardian of their child if the worst-case scenario strikes or who will make financial decisions if they become incapacitated. They aren't avoiding estate planning because they don't care—they're stuck because they care deeply and are afraid of getting it wrong. And what if the plan needs to be changed in the future?

Many people picture estate planning as a maze of legal jargon and documents. The truth is that most plans start with just a few decisions: who will manage finances, who will handle healthcare, and how property will pass.

When What-Ifs Stall The Whole Plan

When we try to predict every outcome, our brains tend to confuse planning with perfection. I once worked with an older couple who owned their home plus two rental properties. Let's call them Charles and Dominique. They came in ready to plan but were visibly anxious—not about the documents, but about their adult kids.

One child had casually mentioned wanting the mountain house. Another assumed they'd inherit the rental near their own home. Charles and Dominique started trying to predict how every decision might land with their kids. What if one child kept their house while the other sold theirs? What if there were arguments about upkeep or value? What if it just felt unfair?

They played out every possible scenario—and each one made them more unsure of how to proceed. So, they delayed working on their plan, again and again.

Eventually, after circling the same questions for months, they made a decision: All real estate would be sold, and the proceeds would be divided equally. No emotional attachments, no arguments over who got what. Just a clear, simple instruction that treated everyone the same and avoided future messes. This may not be what everyone would have done in their situation, but it made them most comfortable.

When Charles and Dominique signed the documents, you could feel the weight lift off their shoulders. The solution wasn't flashy—but it was decisive, and it gave them the peace of mind they'd been chasing for years.

Start Now And Improve As You Go

I understand that many people find making the difficult estate planning decisions to be confusing. The legal system isn't always intuitive. The stakes feel high. And most of us didn't grow up learning how to plan for incapacity, death, or the transition of assets to our loved ones. When we think about it all at once, we get overwhelmed.

Here's the truth most people miss: You don't have to get it perfect and have everything figured out right away.

In fact, those cases are few and far between. Instead, you just get it started and work on improving the plan as you go.

> Here's the truth most people miss: You don't have to get it perfect and have everything figured out right away.

One Step At A Time

One of the best ways to cut through confusion is to break the estate planning process into pieces. Instead of viewing it as one enormous decision, think of it as a series of smaller ones: Who would I trust to act on my behalf if I couldn't make my own financial decisions? What would I want them to know? How about medical decisions? Who is most readily available to assist me now, and who is best suited to stay focused and rational in the event of a medical emergency? Who should receive what I leave behind? Where are my important accounts? What legacy do I want to leave for my family?

Each question brings clarity. Each answer brings structure.

Many people hesitate because they feel like their lives change too often to lock anything in. But the point of estate planning isn't to make one final decision for all time—it's to capture what makes sense for your life right now. Your documents aren't chiseled in stone. They can (and should) be updated as your situation changes. Marriage. Divorce. A new child. A diagnosis. A change in income. You can always revise. But you can't revise something that doesn't exist.

Why Simplicity Comes With Preparation

Another common estate planning roadblock is financial disorganization. I have heard clients say things like, "My accounts are all over the place," or "I'd need to clean up my finances before I even think about a plan." But here's the reality: The longer you wait, the more scattered things tend to get.

Consolidating and organizing accounts isn't just helpful for you; it's a tremendous gift to the people who'll someday need to manage things for you.

In my experience, people are more likely to get organized with their finances if they have a clearer picture of their estate plan. Why can't we handle both issues together and improve the situation? The clarity of the picture we leave for our loved ones helps them when they are in charge of the plan in the future. Once things are organized, the next challenge is making sure others can find what they need when it matters.

> Consolidating and organizing accounts isn't just helpful for you; it's a tremendous gift to the people who'll someday need to manage things for you.

A good plan is like a road map: it shows the final destination and usually the best way to get there.
—H. Stanley Judd

The What, The Where, And The Who

A recent survey found that 52 percent of people don't know where their parents keep their estate documents.[25] That statistic doesn't just reflect confusion—it creates it. And when our loved ones don't understand what documents exist, who's been named in which document, or what their role is supposed to be, it doesn't just lead to stress. It leads to delays, omissions, and mistakes. The worst-case scenario is when multiple family members rush to court with competing wills, all claiming that their version is the "right" one. This is very close to what happened in Aretha Franklin's family after her death in 2018.[26] There are many estate planning lessons we can glean from celebrity estates that went haywire—but I think that would be a topic for another book.

Demystifying The Process

Lawyers should not be the only ones who understand how estate planning works. Yes, the legal side matters. Yes, getting professional guidance can help ensure your plan is solid and compliant with applicable state and federal law.

But you don't have to be an expert to understand the fundamentals.

With the right guidance, estate planning is entirely approachable. And working with an experienced attorney isn't about handing over control; it's about getting the support you need to make informed, confident decisions.

A recent report showed that 12 percent of American adults without a will said they didn't know how to start or found the process too confusing.[27] That statistic appears small at first, but when you look at it relative to the entire population, it amounts to millions of people. If you're feeling that way, you're far from alone. But the key isn't to wait for confidence to show up on its own. It's about taking small steps—and letting clarity come from action.

> You don't have to be an expert to understand the fundamentals.

Clarity Comes From Action

Here are some things I tell clients who feel overwhelmed to help reframe their thinking: You already know more than you think. You know who you trust. You know what matters to you. You know who depends on you. You know which values you want to instill and who will step up to help you if the need arises. That's your foundation. The rest is planning, documents, and organization. All are important, yes, but the process is much more manageable if you take one step at a time.

Overwhelm often fades once you start, but another obstacle tends to appear just as quickly: *presumed cost.* Many people finally gather the courage to begin, only to stop again when they assume estate planning will be too expensive or time-consuming. The truth, as you'll see next, is that planning costs far less than people think. Waiting can be the most expensive decision of all.

But for now, what matters most is this: Feeling overwhelmed is not a reason to avoid planning. It's a reason to begin.

Key Takeaways

Some confusion is normal—complete paralysis isn't.
Feeling confused is a sign that you care, not that you're incapable.

Break it down.
Help yourself plan with a series of small, thoughtful decisions, not a single overwhelming task.

You can revise and improve later.
You can't revise what doesn't exist.

Organization creates calm.
Knowing what, where, and who turns chaos into clarity.

Guidance brings confidence.
Professional help lets you make informed choices with support.

Chapter 8

The Cost Factor

Can You Really Afford Not To Plan?

Fortune favors the prepared mind.
—Louis Pasteur

Even once the confusion clears, many people still hesitate for one very practical reason: cost. Cost is one of the common reasons people delay estate planning. And on the surface, it makes sense. Hiring an attorney. Drafting trusts, wills, powers of attorney, healthcare directives, and other documents. To many, these documents feel like a luxury, something you save for when you have more to protect.

Our daily expenses seem to keep climbing, so we tend to prioritize everyday needs that we see as more urgent than planning. But that logic is exactly backwards.

The Real Cost Of Waiting

When looking at the whole picture, estate planning isn't expensive. Putting it off is. Let me paint a picture for you:

Many Americans plan to pass down property. Nearly 70 percent of property owners plan to gift real estate to their heirs.[28] Homes and land often represent a major portion of family wealth, making real estate one of the most commonly inherited assets.[29]

When someone dies or becomes incapacitated without a plan, the financial fallout frequently exceeds what it would've cost to properly prepare an estate plan. Without a financial power of attorney, your family may need to go to court just to get the legal authorization to pay your bills or manage your care. Without an estate plan, your estate may end up in probate—a legal process that drains time, money, and energy.

> When someone dies or becomes incapacitated without a plan, the financial fallout frequently exceeds what it would've cost to properly prepare an estate plan.

Do the best you can until you know better.
Then when you know better, do better.
—Maya Angelou

How Probate Turns Planning Into Expense

As mentioned previously, probate fees alone can consume 3 percent to 7 percent of an estate's value.[30] The largest part of a typical estate is the home. Home prices vary across the country. According to the National Association of Realtors, in 2025, the median value of a home in the US was $422,800.[31] This means that if you arrange all homes in the

US in order of price, from least to most expensive, $422,800 is right in the middle.

Using the estimated values from above, let's suppose that someone's home and their remaining assets are valued at $500,000 in total. That means probate fees can quickly add up to $15,000 to $35,000 depending on the location and complexity of the case.

Although probate fees and attorney fees vary between states, the financial costs alone are substantial—all money that could've gone to your loved ones.

> Although probate fees and attorney fees vary between states, the financial costs alone are substantial—all money that could've gone to your loved ones.

Time, Stress, And Family Friction

Probate isn't quick. It can take months or even years to resolve a probate estate from start to finish. This also depends on state rules, the complexity of the assets, and family dynamics. Probate timelines are dragged out especially in situations that involve family disagreement and conflict. These issues worsen if the assets aren't titled properly or if there is no estate plan guiding the administration of the estate. Delays in probate cost money and aggravate family dynamics.

When there's no plan, families spend more on legal fees, court costs, document retrieval, and professional services to sort out the mess. In some cases, assets are frozen or tied up until a judge gets involved and issues an order. That means heirs can't access funds for funeral expenses, mortgage payments, or urgent needs.

When Business Planning Is Missing

On the business side, the cost of not planning can be devastating. If you're a small business owner and haven't created a succession or continuity plan, your business—and the people who rely on it—are left vulnerable. Contracts stall. Accounts freeze. Employees quit. Family members disagree. And the entire operation can unravel because a few conversations never happened.

If a business owner doesn't discuss the what-ifs and put a plan in place, the cost of delay adds up. When you don't make decisions as a business owner, someone else has to make decisions that should have been made by you in advance. That friction often leads to conflict, especially when money, grief, and family dynamics intersect. According to one survey, 35 percent of adults say they or someone they know experienced serious family conflict due to a lack of a will or estate plan.[32] And once those conflicts start, they rarely resolve cleanly. Litigation gets expensive. Relationships get fractured. The emotional toll lingers for years.

Planning Failures Can Cost More Than Money

There's also the hidden cost of failing to align your plan with your goals. For example, without the proper legal structure, someone with special needs might lose their government benefits because of receiving inheritance. Or a child who isn't ready to manage money might receive a lump sum with no protections or guardrails to discourage wasteful spending.

These mistakes aren't just financial—they're planning failures. And they're avoidable.

Still, the fear of cost lingers. About 13 percent of Americans without a will say they don't have one because they believe it's too expensive.[33] That's a legitimate concern for many families. But in practice, the cost of a basic estate plan is often far less than people expect—especially when compared against the financial and emotional cost of not having one.

> There's a hidden cost of failing to align your plan with your goals.

What Does Estate Planning Really Cost?

Many people assume estate planning is too expensive—that it's something only for the wealthy or something you put off until later in life. But the reality is, planning can often be far more affordable than people expect, especially when compared to the financial (and emotional) costs of not having anything in place.

Many attorneys offer a range of planning options, depending on your needs. A basic will-based plan typically costs less than a more comprehensive trust-based plan, and many attorneys offer flat-fee arrangements based on the scope of services, so there are no surprises. Other attorneys use an hourly rate fee structure. The fees vary depending on location, so I don't have a detailed, location-specific breakdown for you. I know that people shopping around can find that prices can vary. The fees are specific to each law firm and attorney, but if you do some research and talk to a few attorneys in your area, you will get a sense for the range of costs.

Some people choose to begin with a simple will, while others need a more detailed structure to account for children, real estate, business interests, or blended families. In limited cases involving uncomplicated estate plans, planners can forego a will in exchange for carefully updating account beneficiaries and keeping estate plan costs down. This can work in certain situations, but it isn't the right fit for everyone.

Online platforms may offer low-cost or free templates—but they rarely include the kind of personal guidance that prevents mistakes and may fail to reflect state-specific laws. In practice, these options sometimes result in documents that are outdated, improperly executed, or simply not aligned with the client's actual goals.

So, what is the good news? Learning what your options cost doesn't typically require a financial commitment. Many estate planning attorneys—me included—offer complimentary consultations. That means you get an opportunity to ask questions, understand the scope of the services you need, and get a clear idea of pricing before paying anything at all. The information isn't hidden behind a paywall. It's accessible. And it's worth the conversation.

Yes, planning isn't free. But neither is waiting because of all the hidden financial and emotional costs. And most people are surprised to learn how reasonable the cost of peace of mind can be.

Final Thoughts

Planning doesn't have to be perfect. It doesn't have to be complicated. But it does have to be done while you still have the capacity to make your own choices. That's when the options are open. That's when the costs are manageable. That's when your voice, your values, and your intentions can still be clearly expressed.

So, can you afford to plan? Maybe today feels like the right time. Maybe you still feel unsure. But the real question is this: Can you afford *not* to? The financial, emotional, and relational costs of waiting almost always outweigh the cost of simply getting started.

Now that you've seen the risks of delay and the real-life consequences families face when planning is postponed, it's time to bring the conversation closer to home. Estate planning is not theoretical—it's personal. And it looks different depending on your relationships, responsibilities, and the stage of life you're in.

In the next chapter, we'll explore how planning applies to a wide range of life situations—whether you're single, married, raising children, part of a blended family, caring for a loved one with special needs, aging on your own, or navigating unique family dynamics. No matter your circumstances, planning can be shaped around the people you love and the life you're building.

Before we dive into the documents and tools of estate planning, let's take a moment to see how planning fits into your story.

Key Takeaways

Planning costs less than waiting.
The expense of probate, court filings, and conflict often dwarfs the price of prevention.

Real estate makes delays expensive.
Homes and land are typically the largest estate assets—and the costliest to mismanage.

Conflict is the cost nobody budgets for.
Disputes drain money, time, and relationships.

The price of planning is predictable; the price of delay isn't.
Peace of mind is part of the return on investment.

Chapter 9

Planning For Real Life

How Your Situation Shapes Your Estate Plan

Expect the best, plan for the worst,
and prepare to be surprised.
—Denis Waitley

Estate planning is never just about documents. It's about people, relationships, responsibilities, and the life you're living right now. No two families look the same. No two individuals carry the same worries. And no two planning journeys follow the exact same path.

You may be young and single. You may be raising children. You may be caring for aging parents, navigating a blended family, or managing a household on your own. You may be planning for a loved one with special needs, building a legacy for future generations, or wondering what would happen to a beloved pet if something unexpected occurred. You may be part of the LGBTQ+ community and want to ensure your estate plan recognizes the relationships that matter most to you. And if you're grieving the loss of a spouse or partner, you may simply be trying to take one steady step forward.

Whatever your circumstances, estate planning should reflect your real life—not an abstract idea of what a "typical" family looks like.

This chapter is designed to help you see yourself in the planning process. These aren't legal lessons. They're snapshots of the life experiences people bring with them when they sit across from me, hoping to protect the people they love.

You may find that one of these scenarios fits you perfectly. Or you may see yourself in more than one. The goal isn't to categorize you—it's to meet you where you are and help you understand how planning can make your life easier, clearer, and more secure.

No matter which life scenario reflects your world right now, the most important thing to remember is that estate planning is a personal process—one that grows and adapts as your life changes. The circumstances that shape your plan today may look different in five, ten, or twenty years, and that's perfectly natural. What matters is having a foundation that reflects the people you care about, the responsibilities you carry, and the intentions you want honored. With that foundation in place, planning becomes less overwhelming and more empowering.

> Whatever your circumstances, estate planning should reflect your real life—not an abstract idea of what a "typical" family looks like.

Single Person Without Kids—Choosing Your Team And Protecting Your Voice

Being single without children can offer a lot of flexibility—and it also gives you an opportunity to be especially intentional about planning. Without an obvious default decision-maker to name in a plan, many single adults simply want clarity about who would speak for them in a medical emergency or manage their affairs if they became incapacitated. Some want to ensure the right person—not just the closest relative on paper—has authority to step in. Others want to choose trusted friends or professionals in advance so responsibilities are clearly defined, and no one is caught off guard.

Estate planning gives you the opportunity to choose the people you trust most—whether that's a sibling, a close friend, or someone else you trust in the family. It lets you direct your assets to those who matter to you, whether that's loved ones, charitable organizations, or causes that reflect your values.

Estate planning ensures your voice is heard and your wishes are honored, even when you can't speak for yourself. In many cases, if you decide your estate goes to close family members, friends, or a charity that is near and dear to your heart, you can gain peace of mind by putting your wishes in writing and protecting your legacy.

Single Parent—Focusing On Your Child's Future And Your Own Peace Of Mind

For single parents with young children, estate planning is one of the greatest gifts you can give your children. You carry the full weight of daily decisions and the responsibility for what happens if something unexpected occurs. Many single parents tell me their biggest planning question is this: If something happened to them, who would raise their children—and how can they ensure their children have support and stability?

Planning provides that structure. It lets you give clear instructions about who should step in, how your assets should support your child, and what values you want reflected in their care. A thoughtful plan brings peace of mind, not because you expect the worst, but because you want your child's world to remain steady if life takes a turn.

Married With Children—Protecting Your Spouse, Your Children, And The Life You Built Together

Married parents often feel enormous pressure to get everything right—for each other and for their children. Families in this stage worry about leaving enough clarity for the surviving spouse, balancing fairness among children, and making decisions that reflect their shared values.

Planning offers couples a way to turn those values into instructions. It helps ensure stability for the surviving spouse, support for the children, and continuity for the home and family routines you've built together. It helps ease the burden during grief, reduce uncertainty, and protect the relationships that matter most.

A plan doesn't have to be perfect. It just needs to reflect your intentions and give your family clarity when they need it most.

Blended Families—Clarity, Fairness, And Protecting Every Branch Of Your Family Tree

Blended households often involve overlapping financial, legal, and relational factors, making customized estate planning essential. When one or both spouses have children from prior relationships, planning becomes about balancing loyalty, fairness, and clarity. Without written guidance, even well-intentioned families can experience confusion or conflict.

Estate planning allows you to articulate how you want to support your spouse while also protecting your children. Consider how to ensure that kids on both sides of the family are financially supported, even if something happens to one spouse. It lets you be intentional about sentimental items, family property, and long-term support. Most importantly, it replaces ambiguity with clarity—preventing misunderstandings and preserving relationships during an emotionally difficult time.

Another important note is that many blended families are surprised to learn that most states have laws that protect spouses from being unintentionally or intentionally disinherited. These rules vary from state to state, but generally a surviving spouse is entitled to a minimum share of the estate—even if the estate plan or beneficiary designations leave them with less. This is meant to be a protection for surviving spouses to provide them with some level of financial support after the death of a spouse.

In Colorado, where I practice, for example, a surviving spouse can claim what's known as the spousal elective share of a deceased spouse's estate if they were left with less than that in an inheritance.[34] Other states have similar protections designed to prevent a spouse from being completely cut out of inheritance.

These safeguards are well-intentioned, but they can create unexpected outcomes in blended families if the estate plan doesn't address them. This is why, in addition to thoughtful estate planning, many couples, especially those with children from prior relationships, benefit from a carefully drafted marital agreement (commonly known as a pre-nup or post-nup). These agreements help clarify financial expectations, protect children on both sides, and ensure that everyone understands how assets should be handled if a spouse becomes incapacitated or passes away. Without these agreements, the state law protections I mentioned can affect what happens after one spouse dies.

Ultimately, careful planning becomes a way to honor every branch of your family tree.

Sometimes, the poorest man leaves his children the richest inheritance.

—Ruth E. Renkel

Planning For A Loved One With Special Needs—Providing Stability Without Jeopardizing Support

When you care for someone with special needs, your planning takes on extraordinary significance. Families in this situation often worry about what will happen when they are no longer able to advocate, protect, or guide their differently abled loved ones. They want to provide support without interfering with government benefits or leaving their loved one vulnerable.

A thoughtful plan allows you to preserve access to crucial government benefits, appoint trusted advocates, and provide long-term financial stability. You can also give detailed guidance about care, routines, and the values you want honored. Good planning alleviates uncertainty and helps ensure your loved one is protected, supported, and cared for exactly as you intend.

Pet Parents—Planning For The Companions Who Care For You

For many people, pets are family. That is definitely the case in my family! Our fur babies are precious, like our human family members. Yet, the law classifies them as personal property, no different than our belongings. We certainly want our pets to have a good home with stability and care even if we can't be there to provide it for them. Without an adequate plan, our pets can end up in the wrong hands or with no clear caregiver at all.

Estate planning allows you to choose someone to care for your pets and leave guidance about their routines, medical needs, and comforts. You can also set aside funds or create a trust to ensure their needs are met. Planning for pets isn't indulgent—it's an expression of love and responsibility for companions who bring comfort, loyalty, and joy into your life.

Solo Seniors—Maintaining Independence, Dignity, And Support

Aging on your own can bring pride in your independence—but also concerns about health, finances, and what would happen if you needed help. Many solo seniors worry about losing control or becoming a burden on others.

Planning empowers you to choose who will assist you if needed, how you want decisions made, and what support systems should be put in place. It preserves your wishes, protects your autonomy, and ensures important decisions are entrusted to people who truly understand and care.

Estate planning becomes a way to maintain dignity while thoughtfully preparing for the future.

Leaving A Meaningful Legacy Across Generations

Later in life, many people begin thinking about the impact they want to leave on their children, grandchildren, and even future generations. This isn't just about money; it's about values, traditions, and the hope that the next generation will be better than the last. As the cost of living continues to rise, it is a wonderful gift to future generations to help pay for major life expenses like higher education, purchasing a home, a wedding, or even help with starting a business.

Planning provides a clear way to express that legacy. Whether the desire is to support education, preserve family property, encourage responsible financial habits, or pass down cherished items, a well-structured plan helps ensure your intentions endure. It also protects your own interests by giving trusted individuals the authority to help with financial or healthcare decisions should the need arise.

LGBTQ+ Community—Protecting Your Relationships, Identity, And Intent

For many LGBTQ+ individuals and families, estate planning carries layers of meaning beyond standard documents. It's about creating an estate plan that recognizes and protects the relationships that matter most, including chosen family and trusted loved ones, even when those relationships are not otherwise documented. It helps ensure that the people who rely on you for support are not excluded from important decisions or left without legal protection during a crisis. Many states' laws do not automatically recognize a life partner and do not provide them with the legal protections that spouses enjoy.

Planning allows you to clearly designate who should make decisions for you, who should be informed, and how your assets should be handled. For unmarried partners, tools like cohabitation agreements or (in states like Colorado) designated beneficiary agreements can reinforce and protect your relationship without a marriage. And for LGBTQ+ parents, planning helps protect parental intent and provide clarity for your children's future.

Above all, estate planning becomes a way to honor your relationships and safeguard the life you built.

Small Business Owners—Continuity Through Clarity

Small business owners face estate planning considerations that go beyond their personal lives. Their financial responsibilities, family stability, and the continuity of their business operations are closely connected. When an owner becomes incapacitated or passes away without a plan, the business may stall because no one has legal authority to access accounts, sign contracts, pay employees, or make operational decisions. Even brief interruptions can cause significant disruption and financial losses.

To prevent this, a business can benefit from basic clarity about who is authorized to step in when the owner-operator is not able to manage everyday operations. This often means coordinating personal estate documents with business governance tools such as operating agreements or buy-sell provisions, so authority transfers smoothly and without confusion.

Succession questions also arise. Some owners want the business sold, others prefer it to continue under a partner or family member, and some want it wound down in an orderly way. If there are other owners involved, the prospect of being in business with another owner's spouse or family member may make little sense. Documenting these preferences reduces uncertainty and prevents family members, employees, or colleagues from being forced to make hard decisions without guidance.

A thoughtful, well-coordinated plan helps protect the owner's family, employees, and clients, ensuring the business can continue or wind down in a stable and predictable way.

Widow Or Widower—Rebuilding Stability And Understanding What Comes Next

Losing a spouse reshapes life in profound ways. In the months following a loss, surviving spouses often feel unsteady, overwhelmed, and unsure how to find their way. Estate planning may not be the first thing on their mind—but reviewing their own plan is an important part of rebuilding stability.

This isn't about rushing or making major decisions during grief.

It's about understanding what responsibilities you now carry, what support you may need, and how your goals and priorities may have changed. Updating the estate plan ensures that the surviving spouse remains protected, your wishes are clear, and that the next chapter reflects the new reality.

Moving On

Now that you've seen how estate planning connects to the realities of everyday life, the next step is to understand the tools that make your decisions legally effective. In the chapters ahead, we'll walk through the core components of a solid estate plan—wills, trusts, powers of attorney, healthcare directives, beneficiary designations, and more. You'll learn what each tool does, when it's used, and how the pieces fit together to create a plan that actually works when it's needed most.

Let's open the toolbox.

Key Takeaways

Understanding your life stage brings clarity.
Your plan should reflect your real relationships, responsibilities, and priorities.

One-size-fits-all planning does not fit all scenarios.
Different families and people face different scenarios and have different priorities. The details are where plans succeed or fail.

The right people matter as much as the right documents.
Choosing trustworthy decision-makers is often the most meaningful part of planning.

A good plan meets you where you are.
You don't need perfection—you need a starting point that can grow with you.

Life changes; your plan can, too.
Flexibility is built into the process, but only if a foundation exists.

PART II

Chapter 10

The Will

Huh, Yeah, What Is It Good For?

A goal without a plan is just a wish.
—Antoine de Saint-Exupéry

Please excuse the popular song pun, but I had to use it. For many people, when they finally decide to start estate planning, the will (otherwise known as the last will and testament) is what comes to mind first. Wills have been the default estate planning document for many people when considering estate planning or the transfer of assets after death.

In fact, many of my initial conversations with prospective clients start with, "I would like a will." It's often viewed as the centerpiece of the plan—and sometimes, the only document people think they need or even know about. But while a will plays an important role, it's only one part of a comprehensive estate plan. Some people think a will is both the beginning *and* the end of the planning process. But when you understand what it actually does—and what it doesn't do—you will realize why a will alone is not the *entire* estate plan.

What A Will Really Does

Wills have existed in some form for thousands of years, but their purpose today remains the same: to give structure to your final wishes. A will is a legal document that gives instructions about what should happen to your assets after your death. A will also allows you to name who gets what, identify who should oversee your estate, and nominate a guardian for your minor or incapacitated children. Despite its importance, fewer than one in four American adults currently have a will—a figure that has been declining in recent years.[35]

It's also important to note that the instructions we leave in a will do not work on their own.

> It's also important to note that the instructions we leave in a will do not work on their own.

A Will Isn't An All-Access Pass

A will has no power or authority over your stuff until you've passed away, and even then, it must go through the probate court process before anything can officially be done with it. As a public document, anyone who requests a copy from the court can typically obtain it for a small fee. More on this later, but here's another story to explain my point.

Estelle worked with me shortly after losing her father. Estelle's father, in his final years, decided to simplify everything for Estelle. So, Estelle told me that her father sold his house, closed out old accounts, and kept nearly his entire estate in one bank account. After he passed, Estelle walked into the bank with her father's will in hand, showing that she was the sole heir and had been named to handle everything.

But the bank wouldn't release a dime. The staff were polite, but firm: They couldn't help Estelle even though she presented her father's will. They needed to see a court order officially appointing her as personal representative. The bank, like most financial institutions, isn't allowed to interpret a will. That job belongs to the probate court—and until the court says otherwise, the account stays locked.

This came as a shock to Estelle. But the legal process doesn't run on what felt obvious to her—it runs on legal permissions and authority granted by a court.

That's one of the most common misconceptions I run into: the belief that having a will means you avoid probate.

That is not how it works. A will is a set of instructions for the probate court. It doesn't bypass the court; it invites the court in. Probate is how the court validates your will, appoints your chosen personal representative (also known as an executor), and oversees the process of settling your estate. Depending on your state, that process can be time-consuming, public, and expensive.

Now that I have mentioned the dreaded *p* word, let me briefly explain probate.

> One of the most common misconceptions I run into: the belief that having a will means you avoid probate.

Planning is bringing the future into the present so that you can do something about it now.

—Alan Lakein

Understanding Probate: The Process Behind The Paperwork

Probate is the court-supervised process for settling someone's estate after they die. If there's a will, the court uses those instructions as a guide. If there's no will, the laws of the state decide who inherits and who is in charge. Either way, probate is a legal process—and it moves at the pace of the personal representative and the court system.

It's also important to know that probate is governed by state law, and every state handles it differently. Some states, like Colorado, have a relatively streamlined probate process on paper, but even then, families are often shocked by how long things take.

I always tell my clients that probate is a marathon, not a sprint.

There are assets to collect and safeguard, legal notices to file, waiting periods to observe, debts to settle, accountings to prepare, and final reports to complete before anything is distributed.

In Colorado, the probate process must remain open for at least six months in many cases. This is the earliest the probate process can conclude. Probate typically includes a four-month notice window for creditors to file claims against the estate. This window depends on providing proper legal notice to creditors; it doesn't happen automatically.

In my experience, even straightforward Colorado probates—no disputes, no unusual assets, cooperative heirs—rarely wrap up in under a year. It's not because anything went wrong. That's just the nature of the process. The personal representative is often juggling grief, a family, a full-time job, and the burden of an unfamiliar and sometimes very confusing legal process. Most people called to serve in that role have never gone through the probate process before—and the learning curve can be steep.

> I always tell my clients that probate is a marathon, not a sprint.

What Passes Outside Of Probate

Many people also assume that all their assets automatically go through probate. They don't. Some assets pass outside of probate based on how they're titled or what instructions are on file. For example:

- Joint bank accounts with rights of survivorship typically pass to the surviving account holder without court involvement.
- Retirement accounts, life insurance policies, and other accounts with pay-on-death (POD) or transfer-on-death (TOD) designations pass to the named, living beneficiary outside of probate. If the named beneficiary is deceased, the funds in these accounts may also be stuck in probate.
- Real estate held in joint tenancy will pass to the surviving owner.

Common Misunderstandings About Asset Titling

Not paying close attention to how assets are titled can land us in hot water. I'm referring to one of the most common misconceptions I see people fall for: mistakenly believing an asset is joint when it's not.

I worked with a client I will call Felicia. She believed for many years that she owned her home jointly with her late husband, Felix. It was their family home, and both of their names were on the deed, so Felicia naturally assumed that she owned it.

Years after Felix's death, Felicia tried to sell the house, assuming she had full ownership as the surviving co-owner. But when the deed was reviewed, her realtor discovered Felicia and Felix held the property as *tenants in common*, not *joint tenants with right of survivorship.*

This is a common trap people unsuspectingly fall into—people see two names on a deed and assume that means automatic joint ownership of the whole, when legally, it does not. Both their names were on the deed as owners, but tenancy in common meant that they each owned half of the house. Felix's half didn't automatically pass to Felicia after his death—instead, it became part of his probate estate.

It turned out that Felicia couldn't sell the home without starting probate, becoming the personal representative, and going through the court process. I hated having to give her the bad news and explain that there was no shortcut we could take at that point. It was an expensive and frustrating delay Felicia never saw coming—and it could have been avoided with a clearer plan and proper title work on the deed. The other fact that stung was that Felicia showed me Felix's will. Felix named her to be in charge of his estate and named her as his beneficiary but that will didn't and couldn't get around the language in the deed to their home.

This is why good planning doesn't just rely on estate planning documents—it looks at how assets are owned, titled, and coordinated. Because probate isn't just about the will. It's about the structure behind the plan. And where that structure is missing or mismatched, the default is court. That's why the rest of this book explores ways to reduce your family's reliance on probate—whether through trusts, clear beneficiary designations, or updated titling.

The less our loved ones have to rely on the legal system, the more they can focus on healing, not paperwork.

Limitations Of A Will

Just because wills are not designed to avoid probate doesn't mean wills aren't useful—they absolutely are. They're often the first and most accessible way to express your wishes. But it is important to understand their limitations. Since wills go through the court system, they become publicly accessible documents after they are filed with the court. That means in most circumstances anyone who approaches the court's clerk and pays a small fee can get a copy of the will. It doesn't matter if the person is not family, isn't mentioned in the will, or is a complete stranger.

The fact is that a public document is accessible to the general public. This prospect bothers some people I mention it to, but others don't mind it. If privacy, speed, or avoiding court are priorities for you, a will alone may not be enough.

> The less our loved ones have to rely on the legal system, the more they can focus on healing, not paperwork.

The Essential Role Of The Personal Representative

A well-drafted will serves several critical functions. One of the most important is naming a personal representative. This is the person you trust to carry out your instructions—the one who'll gather your assets, pay your debts, and distribute what's left to the people or charities you've named. Without a will, the court chooses someone based on a priority list written into state law—and that person may not be who you would have wanted.

Naming A Guardian For Minor Children

Equally important for parents of young children is the ability to name a guardian. If you die while your children are still minors and haven't legally nominated a guardian, the court will decide who should raise them. That decision might not align with your values, your family structure, or what's actually best for your kids. And without your input, family members could find themselves in conflict over who should step in—creating stress and uncertainty at the worst possible time.

Testamentary Trusts: A Middle-Ground Option

Another option is a will that includes a testamentary trust, in other words, a trust contained inside a will. This is a type of plan where a trust doesn't exist yet but can be created using the will upon the testator's death under the right conditions. A testator is simply a person who makes a will detailing their wishes regarding their property. You can still use this type of will to control how assets are managed and distributed—especially if you're leaving money to minors or people who may not be ready to handle a lump sum inheritance. A testamentary trust can help keep those funds protected and properly administered under terms you set ahead of time.

For some people, including a testamentary trust in their will is a way to hedge their bets. Maybe they're not ready to go through the time or cost of setting up a trust right now, but they want a backup structure in place just in case. For example, they may be leaving everything to their children—but want the option to create a trust if any of those children are underage, struggling financially, facing legal issues, or dealing with addiction. A testamentary trust allows them to build in flexibility.

This is also a common consideration for families with minor children. If certain conditions exist at the time of the parent's death, the trust will be established by the personal representative of the parent's estate with the court's supervision. If the required conditions are not met, everything can pass to the beneficiaries in the will through the probate process without the need of setting up a trust. It's not a perfect solution—and it doesn't avoid probate—but for some families, it's a practical middle ground between doing nothing at all and setting up a revocable living trust from the start. I will discuss the details of the revocable living trust in chapter 11.

While that might sound like a good solution, keep in mind that because the trust is created by the will, the process still involves probate. A testamentary trust cannot avoid probate because the trust does not legally exist until the court validates the will. And if you want more privacy, more flexibility, or more control during your lifetime, a revocable living trust—which we'll cover in the next chapter—is often the more flexible tool.

Where Wills Can Go Wrong

Wills can also become a source of confusion or conflict when they're written poorly. Vague language, conflicting instructions, or excessive detail can all create problems. I've reviewed wills that attempted to list every single household item with a matching beneficiary—only to leave the family overwhelmed by impossible logistics and unclear intentions. Others use what's called precatory language—suggestions instead of legally binding directives—which creates ambiguity that leads to disputes when some people believe the suggestions are legally enforceable.

Even the best will can be unintentionally overridden if the paperwork on your accounts doesn't match your written instructions. Another issue is people putting too much faith in the will alone, while neglecting other crucial tools like beneficiary designations. Certain accounts, like life insurance and retirement plans, aren't designed to follow the instructions in your will—they are designed to go to the beneficiary you've named on the account itself. The intent is that the beneficiary or beneficiaries would inherit the account even if the will or trust has a different designation for those funds. If the information associated with the account or policy is outdated or missing, your carefully written will can be overruled entirely by an old form that you forgot to check.

A will remains one of the most important documents in an estate plan—but it is not designed to do everything.

It creates structure, names personal representatives, appoints guardians, and expresses your wishes, but it does so through a court process that takes time, requires oversight, and becomes part of the public record.

For some people, that's perfectly acceptable. For others, it raises concerns about privacy, cost, legal headaches, or efficiency.

That's where the next tool comes in. A revocable living trust offers a different pathway—one that can keep your affairs private, avoid probate, and function during your lifetime as well as after your death. If a will is your letter to the court, a trust is your private instruction manual, designed to work seamlessly without inviting the court into the process.

Let's explore how it works.

> A will remains one of the most important documents in an estate plan—but it is not designed to do everything.

Key Takeaways

A will is only one part of the plan.
It provides instructions, but it doesn't handle everything.

A will does not avoid probate.
It guides the court—it doesn't bypass it.

Probate takes time.
Even simple estates require months of court-driven steps and waiting periods.

Some assets don't follow a will.
Beneficiary designations and titling rules can override its instructions.

Wills become public.
Once filed with the court, anyone can request a copy.

Naming decision-makers matters.
A will lets you choose a personal representative and nominate guardians—decisions the court would otherwise make without any input from you.

A will is a start, not the finish line.
It works best when paired with updated titling, beneficiary designations, and other planning tools.

Chapter 11

The Revocable Living Trust

Privacy, Control, And Peace Of Mind

If you don't know where you are going,
you might wind up someplace else.
—Yogi Berra

For people who want to keep their loved ones out of court, a will alone often falls short. Enter the revocable living trust—a reliable tool for control, clarity, and privacy.

I will note that there are many types of trusts, but I will focus on the revocable living trust because it is a very popular estate planning tool and is generally more applicable to many American families. Other trusts and more complex planning tools exist, but we will not be discussing them in this book.

Although trusts feel like a modern legal tool, the underlying concept is ancient. Legal scholars trace the origins of trust-like arrangements back to Roman times, when citizens would use fidei commissum (a form of formalized asset transfer) to leave property to one person who was obliged to hand it over to another.[36] Modern revocable living trusts are built on this same principle: placing assets under someone's management with legally enforceable instructions.

The trust concept also existed for centuries in English common law; however, the revocable living trust didn't become mainstream in American households until the second half of the twentieth century. In fact, federal guidance from 2002 refers to it as "a popular estate planning device in the last several decades."[37]

The appeal is simple:

A living trust allows your estate to bypass the additional time, cost, and strict legal requirements of probate while keeping your estate plan private.

Yet, despite its versatility and how long the revocable living trust has been around, adoption remains surprisingly low. A recent study shows that only 11 percent of American adults have a revocable living trust[38]—an even smaller number than the people who have a will.

I believe this gap is less about need and more about misunderstanding. Some people just don't understand what a trust does or assume it's only for the ultrawealthy or it is too complex for them to work into their estate plan.

Let's clear that up.

A living trust allows your estate to bypass the additional time, cost, and strict legal requirements of probate while keeping your estate plan private.

What Is A Revocable Living Trust?

A revocable living trust is a legal entity that is created during a person's lifetime to hold and manage the person's assets—such as a house, bank accounts, brokerage accounts, and other property. Typically, people looking to establish one of these trusts want to still own and continue to manage all the property they put into their revocable living trust. In a trust, a "trustor" is the name for the original owner of the trust property and the creator of the trust, while a "trustee" is the name for the manager of the trust. The term trustor is also known as "grantor" or "settlor" in some places.

Most people I have spoken with would rather not hand over control of their assets to someone else. In that sense, they play the role of trustee and the trustor at the same time.

This means you are both the manager and the owner of your trust, as long as you choose to be. You retain full control—truly having the benefits of the trust without giving up the practical control of your assets.

The cherry on top is that you are also the primary beneficiary while alive. You can buy, sell, move money, and live life as usual.

Legally speaking, you own and control your revocable living trust, and it owns all your assets. But the real power of the trust shows up when we have to navigate the difficulties of being incapacitated or passing. That's when the successor trustee (someone you've chosen in advance) can step in, without needing court approval or going through the probate process. They can begin handling your affairs or distributing assets according to your wishes as outlined in the trust.

> In a trust, a "trustor" is the name for the original owner of the trust property and the creator of the trust, while a "trustee" is the name for the manager of the trust.

When Does A Trust Work?

Another useful feature of a revocable living trust is that its benefits are not limited to what happens after death.

A well-drafted living trust can (and should) also help us during our lifetime.

If you become ill or disabled, your successor trustee can take over without delay, avoiding the costly and emotionally draining court process of conservatorship or guardianship.

That's what happened to Grace, a retired social worker with no children who set up a trust late in life. When Grace suffered a stroke, her niece—named as Grace's successor trustee—was able to take over immediately. The niece paid bills, coordinated Grace's care, and protected Grace's home and investments without stepping foot in court. Because the trust was funded and properly drafted, no court involvement was required—the successor trustee had proper authority to do what was needed to care for Grace. The plan worked as intended, and the trust worked exactly as it was meant to.

> A well-drafted living trust can (and should) also help us during our lifetime.

How A Trust Works

Unlike a will—which must go through the court system to be validated—a trust operates outside of probate. It's private, faster, and often less expensive for your heirs because it comes with inherently less court-related costs and attorney fees. According to AARP, families using living trusts may experience a simpler, more streamlined transfer of assets and fewer administrative hurdles compared to those relying solely on a will—particularly when the trust is well prepared and properly funded.[39]

Contrary to popular belief, there is no minimum amount of assets someone needs to have in order to establish a revocable living trust. The more assets someone has, the more they can protect and safeguard with a revocable living trust. However, you don't need a fancy house and car to set up a trust.

Change is the law of life. And those who look only to the past or the present are certain to miss the future.

—John F. Kennedy

The Critical Step Many People Miss: Funding The Trust

Even when people go through the effort of setting up a trust, they often miss one of the most important steps: *funding it.*

Creating a trust is like setting up a safe deposit box. You've got the structure, the lock, and even someone in charge of the key—your trustee. But if you never place anything inside, the box remains empty. There's nothing for the trustee to manage, nothing for the trust to protect. Many people assume the document itself transfers property—but the trust agreement simply creates the rules. Funding does the actual work of getting your stuff into the trust you created.

Funding means taking action to retitle your assets—your personal residence, investment property, vacation property, bank accounts, business interests, and investment accounts—into the name of your trust. If an asset stays in your name only and isn't covered by beneficiary designations, it may very well go through probate, no matter how perfect your trust document is.

This is where many people, even those working with attorneys, may fall short. They assume the trust paperwork alone does the job.

The document you create is called the trust agreement, but the trust itself isn't tangible. The trust agreement doesn't transfer your assets into your trust; it sets the rules and guidelines. Even with beautifully drafted trusts, estates will still wind up in probate because the person who set up the trust never took the steps to transfer their assets into the trust. The example below illustrates the importance of a properly funded trust.

The Risks Of A DIY Or Poorly Drafted Trust

Not all trusts work as in Grace's example.

Sometimes, when a do-it-yourself trust goes wrong, the family is left to pick up the pieces.

I once worked with a client whom I will call Dave. Dave was the adult son of a gentleman who passed away. He was one of six children (two were Dave's biological siblings and three were his stepsiblings). Dave's stepmother passed away years earlier, and Dave took over the trust administration shortly after his father passed.

Keep in mind that Dave, who was already very busy at work and with family, now had to carry the full weight of managing his father's estate. Dave's father had attempted to plan by establishing a trust on his own using a template he found online. On the surface, it looked to Dave's father like he had everything in place: a folder of documents and instructions to loved ones. But when Dave brought the documents to me after his father's passing, I noticed many gaps.

The trust was drafted using Washington-specific legal language and required it to be administered under Washington state law, even though Dave's father never lived in Washington. Dave's father was and always had been a Colorado resident. He didn't notice the trust was designed for Washington residents pursuant to their law, and it wasn't customized for him.

State-specific trust statutes govern validity, trustee powers, requirements, and property transfers—and Washington and Colorado differ meaningfully in these areas. I'm not licensed to practice law in Washington, so that was another hurdle we had to overcome.

Worst of all, the trust wasn't fully funded. Although we were able to confirm Dave's father's house was in the trust, the father left his financial accounts, investments, and other assets in his name. There was no formal retitling. The trust had provisions for the property to go to the six children, but the property wasn't placed in the trust. This meant the remainder of his father's estate that wasn't in the trust *still* had to go through probate.

> Sometimes, when a do-it-yourself trust goes wrong, the family is left to pick up the pieces.

Because it was a blended family, the legal gray areas increased friction within the family. The trust nominated Dave as successor trustee, but the will named a stepsibling as the personal representative for the father's estate. It wasn't clear how certain assets were to be handled, and there was an initial power struggle for control over both the estate and the trust.

Dave had to negotiate written agreements with other beneficiaries, some of whom were not cooperative, and others who were openly hostile because they did not believe they would be treated fairly. Even though Dave wanted to follow the terms of the trust and administer the estate in accordance with his father's wishes, his stepsiblings were distrustful due to past disagreements and family drama. They hired attorneys to challenge the administration of the estate.

Ultimately, Dave had to do double duty: navigate the full probate process while also dealing with conflicts with his siblings and stepsiblings and administer the estate using an incomplete trust document that wasn't legally aligned with Colorado law. Only after the probate estate was complete and legal title transferred to the trust were we able to distribute assets from the trust to the beneficiaries and complete the administration process.

Dave did everything right. He was calm, thoughtful, and respectful despite the stresses of the process. But it took us nearly two years before we were done, and we were able to distribute what was left to the beneficiaries. The emotional cost—on top of the administrative burden—was immense. And it was completely avoidable.

Coordinating Your Trust With Beneficiary Designations

Some assets, like individual retirement accounts (IRAs), pensions, 401(k)s, 403(b)s, 457(b)s, aren't retitled into a trust during your lifetime because they can only be owned by a natural person. Still, these types of assets can be aligned with the plan by naming the trust as a beneficiary where appropriate. Coordinating beneficiary designations with your trust is a critical step, especially if you're trying to preserve your legacy and create protections for your spouse, children, or other loved ones. A trust that is not coordinated with beneficiary designations can unintentionally disinherit loved ones or bypass protections you built into the trust.

A trust is only as strong as the work that goes into it. A do-it-yourself template may not account for your state's laws, your family dynamics, or reflect your real-world assets. If it's not properly tailored, funded, and executed, it can cause more confusion than clarity—and leave your loved ones with a bigger legal mess than would have happened without the trust.

Other Benefits

Trusts also offer incredible flexibility. You can specify when and how beneficiaries receive their inherited money and assets. You might want to delay distributions of major assets until a child turns thirty or older or break the gift into multiple stages so they can receive their gift over several age milestones. You can include protections from creditors, divorces, or bad financial decisions.

A revocable living trust shines when your goal is protection and stability for your children. Rather than leaving a single lump sum, you can direct gradual distributions over time, set age-based milestones, and give a trustee clear instructions to use funds for education, healthcare, and support—reducing the risk of impulsive spending or outside pressure. A trust can also benefit special needs beneficiaries without compromising the government-sponsored benefits they may otherwise receive.

Another benefit: you can change it.

A revocable trust isn't set in stone.

You can revise beneficiaries, swap out your successor trustees, or restructure how distributions are made. Most estate planning documents are designed to be amendable. That way, when life changes, your plan can change and adapt to your current wishes.

> A revocable living trust shines when your goal is protection and stability for your children.

Why You Still Need A Will

Some people often ask me whether they still need a will if they have a trust. The answer is yes. Your will acts as a safety net. When you establish a trust, the will serves a support role in your estate plan. It's known as a "pour-over" will, and it catches any assets that weren't moved into your trust (not funded)—either by oversight or mistake. The pour-over will directs those assets to be transferred into your trust after you pass, but that slice of your estate will still go through probate.

Bottom line: A trust isn't just for the wealthy. It's for anyone who wants to keep their family out of court, avoid unnecessary probate delays, and provide a smoother path for their financial affairs to be handled privately and efficiently. It's for anyone who's worked hard to build something—and wants to make sure it transfers with intention, not confusion.

A trust can keep your affairs private and streamlined after you're gone—or if you become incapacitated—but it doesn't operate alone. Every complete estate plan needs a tool that works during your lifetime to ensure financial responsibilities don't fall through the cracks. That's where the financial power of attorney comes in handy. We will cover it in the next chapter.

Key Takeaways

A trust is designed to avoid probate; a will isn't.
Trusts operate privately and without court oversight.

Funding is essential.
A trust only works if assets are retitled or coordinated with it.

DIY documents are risky.
State-specific laws and confusing or incomplete documents can lead to probate and conflict.

Trusts can protect families with unique needs.
Blended families, special needs, and creditor issues benefit from trust structure.

A trust can be flexible.
It can be changed as your life and relationships evolve.

A will is still required when you have a trust.
A pour-over will catches assets that were not added to the trust, but those assets still go through probate.

Chapter 12

The Financial Power Of Attorney

Your Financial Backstop

Plans are worthless, but planning is everything.
—Dwight D. Eisenhower

If a trust is the playbook for what happens to your estate, the financial power of attorney is your quarterback while you're still in the game. It's the document designed to protect you during life, during illness, during incapacity, or during any period when you simply cannot manage your financial affairs on your own.

And yet, despite its importance, it remains one of the most overlooked estate planning tools. According to Merrill Lynch's study with Age Wave, only 31 percent of adults over fifty-five report having a power of attorney in place—far fewer than those who have a will.[40]

That means many people are driving through life with a major blind spot. A will can't help you while you're alive, but a financial power of attorney can prevent your entire financial life from grinding to a halt when you need help the most.

What A Financial Power Of Attorney Actually Does

A financial power of attorney (FPOA), sometimes known as a general durable power of attorney, is a legal document that allows someone else—your agent—to act on your behalf for financial matters. Legally, the person who grants such power to an agent is referred to as the principal. You, as the principal, decide what authority the agent receives.

The authority a principal can grant to an agent can be broad or narrow, depending on the terms of the document itself. This authority can include paying bills, accessing accounts, managing real estate, filing taxes, and more. It's one of the most important tools in your estate planning kit, not because it handles what happens after you die, but because it protects you and puts someone you trust in charge of your finances while you're alive and can't do that for yourself (i.e., incapacity).

People often assume their spouse or adult children can just take over if something happens. But that's not always how it works in real life.

Financial institutions, including banks, investment firms, credit card companies, and others, require legal authorization before they give someone else access to your accounts—even if that person is family. Without a valid, enforceable FPOA, your loved ones may have to go to court and request a conservatorship (sometimes referred to as guardianship), a formal process that is time-consuming, expensive, and public.

The word "durable" suggests that the document is still valid and has effect even when the principal is incapacitated. This is something most people take for granted, but if the document does not include the term, the implication is the authority collapses the moment you lose capacity—the exact moment when it is needed most.

> People often assume their spouse or adult children can just take over if something happens. But that's not always how it works in real life.

What A Financial Power Of Attorney Does *Not* Do

A financial power of attorney has limitations. It does not replace your will or trust, override beneficiary designations, or control what happens to your assets after your death. It typically does not authorize medical decisions—those belong to your healthcare power of attorney—and it does not give your agent automatic authority without proper verification. In other words, a financial power of attorney is a lifetime tool designed to protect you while you are alive and unable to manage your affairs, not an end-of-life document.

Avoiding Court: Why An FPOA Prevents Conservatorships

In Colorado, court intervention for an incapacitated person often means two distinct roles: a conservator for financial matters and a guardian for personal and medical decisions. Other states may combine these responsibilities under a single "guardian" title or use entirely different terminology. Either way, without a valid power of attorney in place, your loved ones may need to ask a judge for permission to make basic financial decisions—and that process can be slow, costly, and deeply personal. We will cover the medical decisions and the healthcare power of attorney in chapter 13.

Why A Well-Drafted FPOA Matters

A properly drafted FPOA helps avoid court when the principal is incapacitated. It gives the chosen agent the authority to step in—immediately if so designated.

But not all FPOAs are created equally. Generic forms often lack the specificity that financial institutions look for. Many financial institutions reject documents that are too vague, outdated, or drafted from generic templates that lack the required statutory language. Others refuse forms that don't clearly spell out authority over specific assets, such as retirement accounts, investment portfolios, real estate powers, or business interests. I've heard of banks declining to honor a financial power of attorney simply because it didn't explicitly authorize the agent to manage certain accounts, or because the document wasn't executed in a manner they were accustomed to.

This is why a carefully drafted FPOA is invaluable—precision matters, and the details determine whether the document works when your family needs it most.

A Real-World Example: Why Precision Matters

Carol had recently gone through serious brain surgery, and during the lengthy recovery process, she was unable to manage her finances. Fortunately, we had just updated her FPOA before the surgery to include specific language allowing her daughter to help her during the recovery, including managing investment accounts, paying her bills, and filing her tax returns.

Carol's daughter was able to handle everything seamlessly—bills were paid, accounts remained in good standing, and her mother's credit and assets stayed protected. Without that document, Carol's daughter would have needed a conservatorship—a process that could have taken months and cost far more than the FPOA.

Do something today that your future self will thank you for.
—Sean Patrick Flanery

Immediate Versus Springing Powers Of Attorney

Some people choose to make their FPOA "springing," meaning it only takes effect if they become incapacitated. Others decide on an "immediate" FPOA, which is valid from the moment it's signed. There are pros and cons to both.

An immediate FPOA is very useful in emergencies—there are little to no delays, and banks or financial professionals that accept the FPOA will honor it right away. The trade-off is that you must fully trust the person you are naming to know when to step in. It's not just about whether you trust the person; it's also about whether they will be able to step in at the right time. They have the legal ability to act on your behalf even while you are still capable and your health does not affect your capabilities.

A springing FPOA works differently: The agent's authority begins only if you become incapacitated. While this offers comfort to some people because it takes the decision of when to step in off your agent's mind, it comes with real-world drawbacks. Incapacity must be proven—often through a doctor's note or multiple certifications by doctors—which may delay getting those doctors' opinions in writing. Those delays could create a bottleneck when swift action is needed, but we must still honor the specific wishes in the FPOA and can't decide to sidestep them. In some cases, institutions even reject springing powers due to ambiguity about when incapacity has been "officially" triggered.

For these reasons, many clients I work with choose immediate authority, because it is the simplest process with the fewest steps—but ultimately, the right choice depends on your comfort level, your family dynamics, and the safeguards you want in place.

Keeping Your FPOA Current

Another common issue people run into is outdated FPOAs that haven't been reviewed in years. Some financial institutions reject documents that are more than a few years old.

If your FPOA hasn't been reviewed in the last three to five years, it's time.

When I sit down with people, I may hear requests to update a will or trust, but I can count on one hand the number of times someone has asked me to update their FPOA without me bringing up the subject. That's a huge blind spot to be driving through life with. Too often, people are more concerned about what happens to their assets after they pass and completely forget to think about how their finances will be kept in check if they need someone to pay their bills during incapacity. An FPOA can keep your entire financial life from unraveling if you become incapacitated.

> If your FPOA hasn't been reviewed in the last three to five years, it's time.

Choosing The Right Agent: It Starts With Trust

Before anything else, your agent must be trustworthy. If there's even a flicker of doubt about their ability to responsibly manage your assets when you cannot, don't name them!

You have to keep in mind that this person will have access to your accounts and your property and have the authority to sign financial documents on your behalf. In most situations that individual does not need someone else's approval to handle your financial affairs, as long as they are named in the FPOA. The rule of thumb I tell people is that if you wouldn't leave them with your checkbook or credit card, they shouldn't be in charge of your finances during a crisis.

Once trust is established, we are not done yet. The next step is choosing the right fit. This role isn't ceremonial—it's hands-on and sometimes high-stress. Ask yourself: Are they available and reliable? Are they organized and financially responsible in their own life? Do they understand your financial situation and wishes? Will they act responsibly, even under pressure? Are they capable of seeking professional advice if needed? Can they manage family dynamics if others get emotional or demanding?

Is the distance from you going to create potential problems? The last consideration is important, but don't fall into the trap of thinking that if the person you want to name lives in another state, you can't name them in your FPOA. In today's world, it is fairly common for somebody out of state to be named as the FPOA agent—it can work.

After you consider this list of questions, you should have a better idea if the person you are considering for the job is the right fit. If you find yourself scratching your head and worried because you don't have any family member or friend that fits the bill, don't fret. There are professionals who can be named in documents to ensure nothing falls through the cracks. They are commonly called professional fiduciaries. You can read more about them in chapter 18.

Now that you have a place to start, here are some other important things you should keep in mind when naming an agent.

Why Birth Order Doesn't Mean Much

Now that we have some of the initial considerations under our belt, let's consider the order of your agents. Too often, people fall into the default trap of naming their adult children in birth order—oldest to youngest. It might be the easiest way to make the decision in the moment of uncertainty, but we need to consider the role closely.

Naming someone as your financial agent is primarily about skill and temperament, not fairness or family politics. As long as the agent is not a minor, age should not be a main consideration. The agent you choose for your FPOA often ends up being the same person you name as trustee or personal representative, because having the same person in charge of all the financial aspects of your estate often makes the most sense.

Pause and consider the responsibilities carefully, and choose someone who can truly handle them.

Next—Have A Conversation Before Naming Agents

This should go without saying—but don't appoint someone to such a serious role without first asking them. Trust me when I say that finding out during a crisis that someone named you in an FPOA is not a fun surprise to be sprung on your loved ones.

Instead of rushing to name them, talk to your prospective agents. Make sure they understand what the role involves. Share your expectations and values. Ask if they feel comfortable taking it on. Do they have challenges or issues in their lives that might make it very hard for them to help you in a time of need?

Estate planning works best when it's not a surprise to you or your loved ones. Clear conversations now can prevent confusion, resentment, and hesitation later. Sometimes, the person you thought was your best option for a financial agent may not be ready to commit to helping you for various reasons. That is information you should be armed with in advance so you can plan accordingly.

Co-Agents Versus Successor Agents—Know The Difference

You can name more than one agent in your FPOA to be in charge at the same time, but it's important to understand how that works in practice.

Co-agents serve at the same time and become your agents by committee. You can require them to act jointly (agree on all decisions and decide together) or independently (either one can act alone even if the other is not available to sign off), depending on the language in your document and what your state law allows.

A successor agent is the backup person you name to act on your behalf if your first-choice agent cannot or will not serve. Think of it as a line of authority. Your first agent has the authority to act first. If that person is unable or unwilling to serve, the next person listed steps into the role. This option typically allows more flexibility in practice. While joint authority might sound balanced, it often causes delays or deadlock—especially if the co-agents don't get along or live in different places. Keep in mind that naming people who are not likely to work well together is a recipe for problems. If it feels like you are making people work together who don't do well as a team, save the headache and name one person first, then another.

Who Is The Backup?

This is the question a good plan should always consider. Ultimately, your plan is only as good as the people you put in place to manage it. If you only have one person named as your agent and that person cannot help when the need arises, what do you really have?

A backup agent only steps in if your first-choice agent is unwilling or unable to serve. It is best practice to name at least one successor agent in every plan, and I often ask my clients to think of a backup to the backup, so they really have a solid plan.

Life changes. People move. Health declines. Having a backup ensures someone can step in when needed—without going to court. If you don't have a successor agent named and your first agent isn't available, the FPOA isn't worth the paper it is printed on.

Your financial life and obligations don't stop just because you're recovering from surgery, suffer from cognitive decline, or are unconscious due to a serious illness. An FPOA makes sure the bills get paid, the lights stay on, and you are taken care of when you can't manage those finances yourself. It's not just a form—it's your financial safety net.

In the next chapter, we'll turn to the healthcare power of attorney—the document that safeguards your wishes, values, and dignity in medical situations when you cannot speak for yourself. The healthcare power of attorney is about clarity, communication, and protecting your values when it matters most.

Key Takeaways

A financial power of attorney protects you while you're alive.
It ensures someone you trust can manage your finances if you can't—something a will or trust cannot do.

Without an FPOA, court intervention may be required.
Banks and financial institutions cannot give family members access without legal authority, often forcing a costly, public conservatorship.

Not all FPOAs are created equal.
Vague, outdated, or DIY forms are frequently rejected, especially by large financial institutions.

Choosing the right agent is essential.
This role demands judgment, availability, financial responsibility, and unwavering trust.

Immediate versus springing authority matters.
Immediate authority avoids delays; springing authority can feel safer but is harder to use in emergencies.

Coordination across your plan is key.
Your agent, trustee, and personal representative often overlap—consistency prevents conflict and confusion.

An FPOA requires periodic updates.
Institutions may refuse old documents; reviewing every three to five years keeps your plan functional.

An FPOA is your safety net.
It keeps your bills paid, your credit protected, and your financial life stable when you're unable to manage it yourself.

Chapter 13

The Medical Durable Power Of Attorney

A Voice When You Can't Speak For Yourself

*Success depends upon previous preparation,
and without such preparation,
there is sure to be failure.*
—Confucius

Most people misunderstand what a medical durable power of attorney actually does. They think of it as an "end-of-life form" or something that only matters when a person is near death. In reality, this document is about helping someone get better—about making sure that, during a medical crisis, someone you trust has the legal authority to speak for you when you cannot. It is a tool of protection, not about "pulling the plug."

A medical durable power of attorney (sometimes known as a healthcare power of attorney) is meant to facilitate care, not stop it. It's not about when you die, but how you're treated while you're still alive but are unable to make healthcare decisions on your own. It allows you to name someone—your healthcare agent—to speak with doctors, understand treatment options, authorize medical decisions, obtain medications, and advocate for you if you're unable to do so yourself. This includes ongoing care, emergency decisions, and day-to-day medical and living needs—everything from understanding a diagnosis to approving a life-saving surgery.

Yet most people still don't have this critical document in place. A National Poll on Healthy Aging from 2020 found that among adults aged fifty to eighty—those most likely to encounter a serious health event—only 46 percent had completed even one advance care planning legal document, such as a medical power of attorney or advance directive.[41] A healthcare power of attorney is another estate planning tool people need in place but often overlook.

The person you name doesn't just have a seat at the table; they are your voice when you can't speak for yourself.

What Makes A Strong Healthcare Agent?

As with an FPOA agent, choosing the right person in charge of your healthcare is critical. But the healthcare role brings its own set of challenges.

The right agent for medical decisions may not be the same person you'd choose to handle your finances. This job is less about numbers and more about judgment, values, emotional strength—and, importantly, availability.

Your healthcare agent may be faced with intense decisions under stressful conditions. They may be in a hospital room, on the phone with specialists, or trying to make choices when your condition is unclear. They may be talking to multiple family members—some supportive, others second-guessing every move—while trying to honor your wishes.

The most important quality here is clarity of purpose. Your agent must be someone who understands what matters to you—not just medically, but personally.

What does quality of life mean to you? What risks would you be willing to take for a chance at recovery? Would you want aggressive treatment or comfort-focused care? Would you prioritize independence, or survival at all costs?

Having these conversations while you are healthy gives your agent the clarity they will need when the unexpected happens. Because when decisions must be made, your agent won't be guessing about how they should proceed. They will understand your wishes and be well-positioned to excel in their role.

> The right agent for medical decisions may not be the same person you'd choose to handle your finances.

Why Availability Matters Even More Than People Think

Medical decision-making unfolds in real time. Physicians expect a healthcare agent who can respond quickly, ask questions, and participate in ongoing discussions. Unlike financial matters—which can often be handled remotely—a healthcare agent may need to be physically present, sometimes for days, weeks, or even months at a time. Long-distance does not automatically disqualify someone from being your healthcare agent, but it does pose practical challenges that should be openly discussed.

Medical decision-making isn't a one-and-done phone call. It's often a series of conversations that unfold over hours, days, or even weeks—each one potentially altering the course of treatment. Your agent may need to visit the hospital, speak with rotating care teams, respond quickly to new information, and coordinate with specialists or palliative care providers. That's not easy to do from far away, so it is not uncommon for healthcare agents to travel and stay with a principal after a serious health event.

So, while a financial agent can often manage tasks remotely and on their own time, a healthcare agent may need to be present, engaged, and responsive in the moment. That's why choosing someone close by—or at least able and willing to show up and stay for an extended time—should be part of the consideration.

Of course, you don't need to disqualify someone who lives far away, especially if they're otherwise the most capable. But if you're leaning in that direction, it's wise to talk through logistics ahead of time and build in a strong backup plan.

Not Everyone Is Built For This Role

Naming the right healthcare agent means looking beyond convenience. Just because someone is close by or a family member doesn't mean they're the best choice.

Can they stay calm under pressure? Will they listen to your doctors and ask the right questions? Can they handle medical language, process complicated information, and act quickly when needed? Are they emotionally capable of making difficult decisions that might go against what others want, but are right for you?

These aren't easy traits to find—and they aren't always found in the eldest child or the person with the most availability.

Some people assume their spouse or adult child will innately know what they want. But knowing and legally acting are two different things. Without a valid document, your loved ones may be left arguing with hospital staff, unsure who has the authority to make decisions, and at risk of being overridden by state default rules or institutional policies.

In Colorado, for example, if no healthcare power of attorney is in place, a proxy decision-maker can be appointed—but only by consensus among family or other interested persons. Other states vary widely, but the takeaway is the same: Without documentation, decision-making becomes slower, more complicated, and more vulnerable to conflict.

Happy families are all alike;
every unhappy family is unhappy in its own way.
—Leo Tolstoy, *Anna Karenina*,
Chapter 1, first line

Co-Agents And Successor Agents

Just like with an FPOA, you can name co-agents for medical decisions—multiple agents can act at the same time. But while this sounds nice in theory, it can create real-world complications when there is disagreement. If one agent wants to pursue one course of treatment while the other disagrees, providers are stuck in the middle. In a medical setting, decisiveness matters.

If you do name co-agents, the document should specify whether they can act independently or must act jointly. Joint decision-making can feel like a safeguard, but it's often a liability when time is short and emotions are high. One unavailable co-agent can grind everything to a halt if medical staff are required to wait for both of them to sign off on a decision.

In medical settings, indecision can be more harmful than an imperfect decision. That is why co-agents, while well-intentioned, often create more problems than they solve. Allowing independent decision-making authority gives an agent the flexibility to make medical decisions if the other co-agent is unavailable to assist.

Another approach is naming an individual as your initial agent, with one or more successor agents listed as backups. That way, if your first choice can't serve, the next person in line is clearly authorized to step in.

> In medical settings, indecision can be more harmful than an imperfect decision.

Don't Forget To Talk To Your Appointed Agents

It's not enough to name the first person you believe fits the mold and move on. You need to talk to them to make sure they are on the same page with you and will be comfortable acting on your behalf. That person should share your values or, at the very least, be able to respect and honor them, even if they disagree. Explain your fears and priorities to them. Tell them how you'd want decisions made if you couldn't speak and make sure they understand your wishes and priorities. This doesn't have to be a heavy conversation—but it does have to happen.

You don't want your agent to be surprised by the appointment or your wishes when they see your healthcare power of attorney for the first time. What's even worse is when your agent is expected to make decisions for you but isn't sure how you would want those decisions made. If you don't communicate your expectations now, your agent is left guessing later—and no matter how close they are to you, that's a difficult place to put them in.

What About Organ Donation?

Not every state has organ donation preferences in a healthcare power of attorney document. In Colorado, you can express your wishes regarding organ and tissue donation in a healthcare power of attorney.

You can authorize organ donation or even the donation of your body for medical research or educational purposes. When considering body donation it's important to decide if a delay in obtaining your remains will be uncomfortable or difficult for your loved ones to handle. If you agree to body donation, it may take a year or longer before remains are returned to family. Ultimately, it is your body and your decision—we don't need to leave it to our agents. Either way, documenting your intent relieves your loved ones of a burden and gives medical professionals a clear directive in time-sensitive situations.

Some people include specific limitations—like donating for transplant but not research—while others express more general preferences. There's no one right answer, but your healthcare agent and medical staff should clearly know what that answer is for you.

Supplemental Medical Planning Documents

While the healthcare power of attorney is the strongest way to ensure someone you trust can make medical decisions for you, it's not the only form that shows up in healthcare settings. Many hospitals and care facilities offer or refer to additional documents that can express medical wishes or allow someone to temporarily make medical decisions for a person without a healthcare power of attorney in place.

Five Wishes—Purpose And Limitations

One example is the Five Wishes form, created by the nonprofit Aging with Dignity.[42] It's a widely used document that combines the appointment of a healthcare agent with personal care preferences and values. Designed to be more conversational than clinical, it walks individuals through choices about pain management, comfort, emotional support, and end-of-life care, all in one place. It's legally recognized in most states, though some may require additional documents or modifications to meet local requirements. Because of its ease of use and emotional accessibility, it's often distributed by hospices, senior organizations, and some medical providers.

MOST/MOLST/POLST

Another form you may come across in hospitals or long-term care settings is the MOST form (Medical Orders for Scope of Treatment)[43]—this is sometimes known as a MOLST form (Medical Orders for Life-Sustaining Treatment)[44] or POLST form (Provider/Physician Orders for Life-Sustaining Treatment) in some jurisdictions.[45]

In Colorado and many other states, these forms are available to help patients clearly express their treatment preferences in the absence of a healthcare power of attorney and an advance healthcare directive—especially regarding life-sustaining measures such as resuscitation, intubation, or artificial nutrition.

While these forms are technically medical orders, they are often initiated by a patient (or their representative) in collaboration with a healthcare provider, particularly when a medical power of attorney has not been prepared. Once completed, the MOST form becomes actionable instructions to healthcare teams.

These Don't Replace A Healthcare Power Of Attorney

Although the forms discussed above are especially common among elderly individuals, those hospitalized, or those living in assisted care environments, they are not replacements for a healthcare power of attorney or a living will. MOST forms do not name any agents—they provide direction.

And what about documenting your personal choices for end-of-life treatment—whether to continue life support in extreme circumstances, or not? That's the focus of the living will, which we'll cover in the next chapter. But first, let's look at HIPAA releases.

Why A HIPAA Release Matters More Than You Think

One of the most overlooked but essential parts of the healthcare power of attorney package is the HIPAA release. HIPAA stands for Health Insurance Portability and Accountability Act—a federal law that protects the privacy of your medical information and strictly limits who can access and discuss it without your written consent.[46] Remember when you last visited your primary care physician? Did the staff ask you to complete a form indicating whom you authorize them to contact with your confidential medical information? That is called a HIPAA release. HIPAA is meant to keep our medical information confidential, but if we are not adequately prepared, it can also prevent medical providers from releasing information to our loved ones. Clients often ask why they need one—especially since they sign HIPAA release forms all the time at medical appointments.

The HIPAA release form you sign at your doctor's office applies only to that provider and often times only for that visit. In an emergency—especially at a hospital where you've never been treated—your agent may be blocked from receiving updates or discussing your condition unless you've signed a universal HIPAA release as part of your estate plan.

Imagine this scenario: You're unconscious after an accident, you're being treated at a hospital by a doctor you've never seen before, and your appointed healthcare agent wants to speak with your care team or access your records. That hospital has no existing HIPAA release on file—and no legal right to disclose anything to your healthcare agent.

This is not a pleasant scenario for our loved ones, so let's try to avoid it altogether. Having a general HIPAA release form as part of your estate plan gives your agents standing permission to talk to any provider, any hospital, and any medical record system—no scrambling required.

Who Should Be Named?

A HIPAA release doesn't just have to name your healthcare agent. It can—and often should—include trusted family members or others you want to stay informed, even if they're not the primary decision-maker. Some people want children, siblings, or close friends to be able to get medical information, even if they are not the ones making the decisions, for support and communication.

Just be thoughtful. The release grants access to information, not decision-making authority—but it still reveals sensitive medical information. Anyone listed should be someone you trust.

What A Healthcare Power Of Attorney Does *Not* Do

A healthcare power of attorney is essential, but its authority has limits. It does not give your agent control over your finances—that role belongs to a financial power of attorney. It is not meant to override written end-of-life instructions, such as a living will or documented treatment orders like a MOST or POLST form. It also doesn't grant automatic access to your medical information unless paired with a HIPAA release or unless the healthcare power of attorney contains legal language that would qualify as a HIPAA release.

While a medical power of attorney empowers your agent to speak for you when you cannot make your own decisions, healthcare providers may still require proof of authority—such as reviewing the signed document or verifying its validity—before they follow your agent's instructions.

In short, a healthcare power of attorney guides care during your lifetime, but it works best when supported by the other components of a complete estate plan.

Your medical durable power of attorney ensures someone you trust can speak for you when you can't speak for yourself—but it does not address what should happen in the most serious medical situations. When treatment decisions become questions of life support, artificial nutrition, or end-of-life care, your healthcare agent still needs clear guidance.

That is the role of the living will.

In the next chapter, we'll look at how a living will works alongside your medical power of attorney to provide direction during the most difficult medical moments, reduce uncertainty, and protect your loved ones from the weight of guessing what you would have wanted.

> A healthcare power of attorney guides care during your lifetime, but it works best when supported by the other components of a complete estate plan.

Key Takeaways

A healthcare power of attorney protects you during life.
It authorizes someone you trust to make healthcare decisions when you cannot.

Choosing the right healthcare agent is critical.
This role requires judgment, emotional steadiness, and willingness to advocate under pressure.

Availability and proximity can affect outcomes.
Medical decisions often unfold in real time and may require rapid responses.

A HIPAA release is a practical necessity.
Without one, your agent may struggle to access information needed to act.

Without a healthcare power of attorney, state default rules take over.
That can lead to delays, confusion, or disputes during a crisis.

A healthcare power of attorney works best as part of a coordinated plan.
It complements—rather than replaces—living wills and medical orders like MOST/POLST.

Chapter 14

The Advance Directive

When Treatment Decisions Become Life-And-Death

An ounce of prevention is worth a pound of cure.
—Benjamin Franklin

Let's be honest: This is one of the hardest parts of estate planning. Not because it is legally complex, but because it forces people to picture a scenario no one wants to imagine—lying in a hospital bed, unable to speak, while loved ones are asked to decide whether continued life support makes sense when recovery is no longer expected. In my experience, clients often begin this conversation tense and leave visibly relieved—because once the decision is made, the fear of the unknown softens into clarity.

Many times I see clients come into this discussion with anxiety about the decision and wanting to move on from the topic as soon as possible. This is an understandable reaction.

Deciding when life support should be stopped is inherently uncomfortable.

It's emotional. And that's exactly why it matters so much for us to make our own decision well before it may be needed.

The advance healthcare directive, more commonly known as a living will, is the document that gives your medical team and your loved ones a clear set of instructions for what kind of care you want during end-of-life situations if you are unlikely to recover. Some of my clients jokingly refer to this as the "pull-the-plug" document.

A living will is meant to apply under specific medical circumstances—generally when you cannot communicate, and you are in a terminal condition or a persistent vegetative state (or other qualifying condition defined by state law). It is designed to guide decisions about life-sustaining treatment when recovery to meaningful cognitive function is not expected.

> The advance healthcare directive is the document that gives your medical team and your loved ones a clear set of instructions for end-of-life situations.

What A Living Will Actually Does

A living will gives written instructions about the types of life-sustaining treatment you do or do not want under specific medical conditions when you cannot express your wishes yourself. It does not appoint a decision-maker—that is the role of your medical power of attorney.

Living wills typically apply in two categories of circumstances: (1) a terminal condition, where death is expected with limited or no meaningful treatment options, and (2) a persistent vegetative state, where consciousness and brain activity are not expected. In either case, the directive only becomes relevant when the person cannot communicate their wishes. The important distinction to draw is that if someone is lucid and suffering from a terminal illness, the living will doesn't take effect until and unless that person is no longer able to communicate (typically this involves a loss of consciousness).

What A Living Will Does *Not* Do

Bear in mind that a living will is not a substitute for a palliative care plan. Comfort care should always be addressed through a person's care team and healthcare agent, but the living will's focus is narrower: whether to continue or discontinue life-sustaining interventions when the legal and medical criteria are met.

A living will is an important guide, but it has limits. It does not typically appoint a decision-maker or give anyone legal authority to act—that role belongs to a medical durable power of attorney. It is also not triggered by routine medical situations, temporary incapacity, or treatable conditions where meaningful recovery is expected.

A living will does not replace medical orders such as a do-not-resuscitate order (commonly referred to as a DNR) or MOST/POLST form, and it does not prevent comfort-focused care; pain control and dignity-based care should continue regardless of whether life-sustaining treatment is continued or discontinued.

Finally, a living will cannot guide anyone if it cannot be located or if your loved ones have never discussed your values, which is why access and communication are just as important as signing the document.

About Giving Guidance

Some people hear the term *living will* and mistakenly assume it's about giving up. That's not what it is. The purpose of a living will is to turn your values into instructions—so your loved ones are not forced to guess in the dark. "Here's what I would want if there's nothing left to do that would restore me to a meaningful quality of life."

The goal of a living will is not to speed up death. It's to protect a person from being kept alive through invasive or unwanted interventions that do not serve their wishes or preserve their dignity.

The Toll On Families Without A Living Will

When there is no living will, the burden falls entirely on loved ones. They're left trying to guess what you would want, sometimes while sitting at your hospital bedside, surrounded by monitors, machines, and medical staff seeking a decision. In those moments, families don't just feel stress; they feel guilt. And worse, they may not agree.

Even the most loving families struggle with this. One child may say, "She wouldn't want to live like this," while another says, "We have to keep trying." The emotional stakes are sky-high.

A clear directive spares your family from that impossible position and frees them to simply be there for you and each other.

A living will provides family members with critical guidance and is designed to take the family argument out of the equation. Let's give the family time to visit, talk to doctors, understand the condition, and begin to cope with the situation, instead of giving them something to argue about with life-or-death decisions.

The more informed we are, the more we understand and the better we're able to protect ourselves, our family, and assets.

—Spencer Sean

The Terri Schiavo Case: A National Wake-Up Call

One of the most well-known and heartbreaking public examples of life-sustaining treatment without a living will was the case of Terri Schiavo.[47]

In 1990, Terri Schiavo, a twenty-six-year-old woman living in Florida, collapsed after her heart stopped, depriving her brain of blood flow and oxygen. Terri's brain was irreparably damaged, and she fell into a persistent vegetative state. Despite efforts to improve her condition, doctors were unable to help her.

For over a decade, her husband and her parents were locked in a fierce legal battle over whether to continue or withdraw life support. Her husband believed she would not have wanted prolonged life support without awareness or meaningful recovery; her parents disagreed.

There was no written document confirming her wishes, and the court cases focused on what Terri had said in the past.

What followed was a prolonged and painful public dispute—involving multiple courts, governors, Congress, and even the president at the time. Terri remained in a persistent vegetative state for fifteen years until her death in 2005.[48]

Her case sparked a national discussion and highlighted the devastating consequences of the absence of written instructions.

Around the country, states continued to refine advance directive laws over time. In Colorado, for example, the legislature significantly revised its advance directive statute in 2010, modernizing the framework and expressly recognizing persistent vegetative state as a qualifying condition—leaving medical determinations to physicians rather than courtroom battles.[49]

It Doesn't Have To Be Complicated

A living will can be short. Some people choose to discontinue life-sustaining treatment as soon as the necessary medical criteria are met.

Others request a defined period of continued treatment to allow family and friends time to visit and come to terms with the situation. What matters is not the length of the document, but the clarity of the guidance it provides.

In Colorado and many other states, statutory forms are available that cover essential decisions, including whether to continue artificial life support, artificial hydration, or nutrition (e.g., ventilators and feeding tubes) in situations covered by the directive. Many people choose to create one with their estate planning attorney to ensure it integrates properly with the rest of their plan—and avoids conflicting instructions.

How Is A Living Will Different From A Do Not Resuscitate Order?

This is one of the most common areas of confusion. A DNR is a medical order, not an estate planning document.[50] I have been asked by clients to prepare a DNR, and I had to decline because I'm not a medical doctor. A DNR is not the same as a living will, and it's important to know how they differ.

A DNR tells healthcare professionals not to administer CPR or advanced life support if a person's heart or breathing stops. It is created after consultation with a physician and is signed by a medical professional.

In many states, it must be posted clearly or worn as a bracelet or necklace to be effective in emergency settings—especially outside the hospital. Unless medical personnel are aware of a DNR, they will do everything in their power to administer lifesaving procedures.

In some cases, a DNR is also reflected in a MOST/POLST form, which translates a patient's preferences into medical orders that travel across care settings.

A living will, on the other hand, dictates if life-sustaining procedures should be continued in the event of a terminal condition or persistent vegetative state—and if so, for how long.

These different tools can and often should exist together, especially if someone is adamant and has given careful consideration to the matters of life support and resuscitation, but neither of these documents replaces the other.

Don't Wait For Later

Too many people think a living will is only for the elderly or those diagnosed with a terminal illness. But many of the hardest medical decisions arise from unexpected emergencies—strokes, brain injuries, or traumatic accidents—where there's no time to draft new paperwork or figure out what someone probably would have wanted.

Creating a living will now gives you the opportunity to decide while you're clearheaded and to protect the people you love from having to carry that burden alone.

A living will isn't about giving up control. It is about keeping it by putting your values in writing before a crisis forces your loved ones to make decisions for you. A medical power of attorney gives someone authority to speak for you during treatment. A living will gives that person guidance when the question becomes whether life-sustaining interventions still serve your definition of dignity and meaningful recovery.

> Creating a living will now gives you the opportunity to decide while you're clearheaded and to protect the people you love from having to carry that burden alone.

Key Takeaways

A living will provides end-of-life instructions.
It guides care when you cannot communicate and recovery is not expected.

It does not appoint a decision-maker.
Authority typically comes from your medical power of attorney; the living will provides guidance.

It reduces conflict and guilt for loved ones.
Clear instructions prevent guessing during crisis decisions.

A living will is different from a DNR.
A DNR addresses resuscitation; a living will addresses ongoing life-sustaining treatment.

Comfort care still matters.
Choosing limits on life support does not mean choosing no care.

Chapter 15

Planning For The Disposition Of Your Remains

To be prepared is half the victory.
—Miguel de Cervantes

Much like the living will, deciding what happens to someone's remains is not a topic most people enjoy discussing. But it can become one of the most emotionally charged moments a family faces, especially when there is no clear direction.

When instructions are missing, even close families can find themselves in conflict over what a loved one would have wanted. A short document outlining your wishes in a clear, organized manner can spare your loved ones unnecessary heartache.

In Colorado, this tool is called the declaration of disposition of last remains. Other states use different names or fold similar language into other planning documents. Regardless of the format, the goal is the same: A person should have the final say over what happens to their body after they pass away, and the law should make it clear who has the authority to carry out those wishes. This is referred to as the Right of Sepulcher in the US.[51]

What Is The Declaration Of Disposition Of Last Remains?

The declaration of disposition of last remains allows a person to put instructions in writing about what should happen after death and, just as importantly, who is authorized to carry out the responsibility of handling our remains. In Colorado, a declaration can specify the disposition of last remains, appoint the person who directs the disposition, and address ceremonial arrangements and who directs those arrangements.

That can include preferences such as burial or cremation, and it may also include other methods depending on what is permitted and available in the person's jurisdiction at the time. Colorado, for example, has also authorized natural organic reduction and water cremation.

The point is not to overwhelm anyone with options.

The point is to reduce uncertainty and ensure your wishes—and the right decision-maker—are clearly documented.

> The point is to reduce uncertainty and ensure your wishes—and the right decision-maker—are clearly documented.

A Story That Didn't Have To End That Way

Consider what happened to two siblings, Jasmine and Isaac. They had just lost their mother. Now, Jasmine and Isaac were facing a difficult decision: burial or cremation.

Jasmine said her mother had confided to her that she wanted to be buried next to her parents. Isaac was adamant that their mom had changed her mind later and wanted to be cremated, saying she even mentioned wanting her ashes scattered.

Neither sibling was careless with the decision nor trying to "win." Both were acting from love and from the information they believed was true.

The problem was that their mother had never written down her wishes, and she had shared different wishes in separate conversations with her children at different times in her life. These conversations were both in private, with no witnesses and no paper trail.

There was no way to know which version reflected her final wishes.

After a long and emotionally draining debate, Isaac moved forward with cremation. And long after the service was over, Jasmine continued to resent her brother for, in her mind, not respecting their mother's wishes.

All of it could have been avoided with a short document that replaced uncertainty with clarity.

> All of it could have been avoided with a short document that replaced uncertainty with clarity.

Why A Will Isn't Always Enough

Some people assume these instructions can simply be placed in a will. Sometimes they can—but practically speaking, a will is often not the first document family members reach for, and it may not be located or reviewed until after time-sensitive decisions have already been made. Funeral homes, hospitals, and coroners often need direction quickly.

That's why a standalone declaration is powerful. It's shorter and easily accessible to a family after a death. And in Colorado, a standalone declaration is fully enforceable under the law.[52] Another benefit is flexibility: If your wishes change later, updating a declaration of disposition of last remains is usually easier—and often less expensive—than revising your will.

The Practical Piece Most People Miss: Make It Easy To Find

This document only helps if the right people can access it when it's needed. A practical best practice is to keep it with other grab-and-go information—your estate planning binder, a clearly labeled folder at home, or a secure digital vault—and to give a copy to the person you appoint to carry out the instructions. Some people also provide a copy to a trusted family member or keep it with their other healthcare and emergency contacts. The goal is simple: no scrambling, no guessing, no delays.

Don't wait. The time will never be just right.
—Napoleon Hill

Final Thoughts

Planning for the disposition of your remains isn't grim—it's compassionate. It protects your loved ones from uncertainty and conflict, and it gives them the freedom to focus on grieving and honoring you rather than trying to guess your wishes.

The declaration of disposition of last remains may be one of the shortest documents in an estate plan, but it can have an outsized impact on what your family experiences in the days immediately after loss.

These core tools—your will, trust, powers of attorney, healthcare directives, HIPAA releases, and disposition instructions—create the foundation of a working plan. With your core estate planning tools in place, the next step is making sure the plan works the way it's supposed to in real life. The core tools are only the beginning. Next, we'll turn to beneficiary designations, simple account instructions that can override your plan if the beneficiary designations are outdated or inconsistent.

Key Takeaways

These instructions are time sensitive.
Families often must make decisions within days, well before the probate process typically starts.

A separate declaration reduces confusion.
It provides clear written direction when emotions are high and time is short.

Written instructions reduce family conflict.
Clarity prevents loved ones from having to guess—and disagree—about your wishes.

Access matters as much as signing.
A document no one can find cannot protect your family when it is needed most.

PART III

Chapter 16

Outdated Beneficiary Designations

Unintended Consequences

Measure seven times, cut once.
—Russian proverb

American retirees, financial advisors, and estate planners are watching what many call the greatest intergenerational transfer of wealth in history.

Credible projections estimate that tens of trillions of dollars will pass to heirs and charities over the coming decades, often cited at roughly \$84 trillion by 2045,[53] with some estimates climbing above \$100 trillion later in the 2040s.[54]

That transfer won't happen through wills alone. Much of it will move through retirement accounts, life insurance, and investment accounts—assets that are frequently controlled by one deceptively simple tool: the beneficiary designation.

These staggering figures underscore the importance of having every piece of your estate plan—even beneficiary designations—figured out.

The Form That Can Override An Estate Plan

A beneficiary designation is the form you complete to name who should receive certain assets, such as retirement accounts, life insurance policies, or workplace benefits, after your death. This typically involves completing a form that asks you to name beneficiaries—the person or persons who will receive the ownership rights to the account if you die. And while it may seem like a minor detail when we are rushing to complete the paperwork, an outdated or poorly considered beneficiary designation can completely hijack an estate plan.

Consider how easily this can go wrong:

- An ex-spouse inherits a retirement account because the designation was never updated after the divorce.
- A parent unintentionally excludes a child because he listed one child's name and left out the other.
- A long-term partner is left financially exposed because their partner forgot to update an old designation—naming a sibling or parent—from an earlier chapter of their life before meeting the partner.

These aren't rare mistakes. They're common oversights discovered only after it's too late to fix them.

> An outdated or poorly considered beneficiary designation can completely hijack an estate plan.

What Beneficiary Designations Control

Here's the key thing to understand: Beneficiary designations operate outside the will and trust. They are contractual obligations that a financial institution agrees to follow in the event of the account owner's death. That means the asset passes directly to the individuals or entities named on the beneficiary designation form, even if the will or trust indicates otherwise. If your will says your estate, including all your retirement accounts, should be divided equally among your three children, but your IRA lists only your oldest child as the beneficiary, that one child gets the entire account.

Financial institutions are required to transfer the asset to the beneficiary listed. There is no obligation or ability for them to check whether your estate plan says something different, and in many cases, financial institutions have no idea about your estate plan. The beneficiary designation on file is what financial institutions follow, and they do not deviate from this practice without a court order to the contrary.

The Real-World Consequences

I regularly work with clients who are shocked to learn how easily their estate plan can go wrong when it conflicts with their beneficiary designations.

To illustrate this, I will share another story. James finalized a will that carefully divided assets among several family members, including his spouse, Kendra, but James never updated the beneficiary forms on his life insurance policy and online investment accounts. The problem was that James's accounts named Kendra and a charity as beneficiaries and left out all the other people named in James's will.

Despite what the will instructed regarding his property, the accounts were paid only to the named beneficiaries. James's other family members were understandably upset since they assumed the will controlled all of his money, including these accounts. But beneficiary designations are not adjusted by what is written in a person's will. Financial institutions are required to pay those accounts according to the beneficiary designations on file, regardless of what the will says.

When Young Children Are Named Directly

Another common issue occurs when minor children are named as direct beneficiaries of large financial accounts. Most people assume naming their child is straightforward, but in reality, minor children cannot legally inherit large assets outright. If a minor is listed as a beneficiary and the parent dies, the funds often cannot be accessed until a conservatorship (or guardianship, depending on your state's law) is established through the court. In other words, the account isn't owned by the child in any practical sense until a court grants supervision and allows management of the account.

Relationship Changes Don't Update Forms

Unmarried couples face a different kind of risk. Single people without children tend to name their family members as beneficiaries on their accounts. When a life partner or serious long-term relationship develops, many people forget to update their beneficiary designations to name the partner. If beneficiary designations aren't updated to reflect the current relationship, a partner may be completely excluded, especially because unmarried partners usually don't receive the same default protections under intestacy laws that spouses do.

Those oversights can leave someone with little legal leverage and immediate financial issues.

I've also seen married couples name each other as the sole beneficiaries on their life insurance policies. But after one spouse passes, the surviving spouse forgets to name a new beneficiary. If that surviving spouse dies without updating the beneficiary designation, the policy typically does not automatically go to any beneficiary since no living beneficiary was listed. Although some life insurance companies include default beneficiary language, many do not, and these cases often end up in probate after the monies are paid into the surviving spouse's estate. It all becomes subject to the court probate proceedings to determine the appropriate recipient.

> If beneficiary designations are outdated, the estate plan isn't complete.

The Weakest Link Problem

All of these scenarios share a common theme: People meant well but did not understand the significance of beneficiary designations or the need to keep them up to date. When people assume their will will control, or that the right people will benefit, plans can go haywire. Remember that beneficiary designations are designed to enforce and pay out to specifically listed people, even if it has been many years since the beneficiary designation was entered.

This is why I tell clients that their estate plan is only as strong as the weakest piece. If the plan isn't comprehensive and beneficiaries are not updated, we will run into unintended consequences. If beneficiary designations are outdated, the estate plan isn't complete. And these mistakes often go unnoticed until it's too late to fix them.

Let our advance worrying become
advance thinking and planning.
—Winston Churchill

Contingent Beneficiaries: The Backup Plan

Clients often ask me if naming a contingent beneficiary is necessary. There is no universally accepted answer here, but frequently the answer is yes. Oftentimes, it is wise to consider the possibility of that backup plan. If your primary beneficiary passes away and there is no one else named as a beneficiary, the asset may revert to your estate and go through probate. Ironically, the designation was meant to avoid this issue, but it can't do its job because it was not kept up to date.

You don't need a lawyer to update your beneficiary designations—generally, you can do so yourself by contacting the bank, your employer, your financial advisor, and the financial institution where your money is held. But you do need intention. It is on all of us to double-check that the paperwork on file reflects our current wishes and is aligned with our plans.

Final Thoughts

Estate planning isn't just about signing the right documents. It's about making sure every moving piece works together as part of a larger plan. When beneficiary designations are outdated, they don't merely create inconvenience; they can completely override your intentions. Remember to measure carefully here, because this is one cut that can't be undone after the fact.

Key Takeaways

Beneficiary designations can control major assets.
They generally take precedence over what a will or trust says because they function as instructions on file with the institution.

Old designations don't automatically "adjust" to life changes.
Divorce, remarriage, and new relationships need to be reflected in your beneficiary designations.

Naming a minor can trigger court involvement.
Minor children usually cannot receive and control large assets outright without supervision.

Contingent beneficiaries are part of risk management.
When no backup is named, assets may default into probate or into outcomes the owner never intended.

Beneficiary reviews should be routine, not reactive.
A quick check after major life events prevents consequences that can't be fixed after death.

Chapter 17

Communicating With Your Loved Ones

Avoiding Unwanted Surprises

Plans are only good intentions unless they immediately degenerate into hard work—and communication.

—Peter Drucker

If you think that your estate planning journey is just getting the right documents in place, I have to burst your bubble here. That is only half of the battle. The other half of the challenge is ensuring you communicate with the people you love. This helps them feel more ready to step in and follow the plan you created when the time is right.

Too often, the people who should know the details of our plans and wishes are left in the dark about these important decisions and roles because we did not want to raise this serious subject. We're willing to invest time and money in wills, trusts, and powers of attorney—but we hesitate to communicate what we've done and who we are relying on to ensure our plans are put into action. Sometimes we don't want to communicate our wishes because of privacy concerns. Sometimes it's fear of conflict. Sometimes we worry that once we say it out loud, we won't be free to change our minds later.

Silence Creates A Vacuum

But here's the hard truth: The real conflict under the surface isn't caused by the conversation—it's caused by the lack of one.

I've seen too many situations where families fall into conflict, not because of the plan that existed, but because no one knew what the plan was before a loved one died. Surprises breed suspicion. Confusion opens the door to resentment.

Even legally flawless documents can fail if no one understands the reasoning behind them.

> Surprises breed suspicion.
> Confusion opens the door to resentment.

Why Communication Matters

Discussing your estate plan does not require you to reveal every detail about your finances. It means creating a basic understanding of your wishes, your values, and the roles people are being asked to take on. Telling your children that you've appointed one sibling to serve as trustee isn't about asking permission—it's about giving clarity, so your children don't find out after the fact and wonder why. It's about framing your decision in the context of logistics, not favoritism.

These conversations also give your loved ones time to ask questions, express concerns, and understand their future responsibilities. They help ensure that your fiduciaries—your personal representative, trustee, agent under a power of attorney—aren't blindsided or overwhelmed by a responsibility you left for them. The people you name in your estate plan give your plan context, humanity, and resilience.

It Doesn't Have To Be One Big Talk

Start small. Let your trusted people know you've started the planning process. Mention that you plan to put documents in place and that your goal is to ease stress, not to create it. Share the location of your documents and the name of your attorney if you use one. Schedule a conversation (or several conversations) when everyone is calm—not during a holiday meal or family emergency.

Every family dynamic is different. In some families, group conversations are best. In others, one-on-one discussions create more transparency. Don't force the conversation into a mold it doesn't fit—adapt the approach to your family's communication style. If things are complex or you anticipate pushback, consider inviting a neutral professional (like your attorney or a financial advisor) to help facilitate.

One important caveat: Communication should be safe.

Some families have complicated dynamics, and sometimes sharing details creates anxiety, pressure, or conflict that doesn't need to exist. If trust is shaky or if there are concerns about exploitation or emotional volatility, it may be more protective to keep the conversation at a high level. A plan can still work beautifully when the right people know the right information, even if everyone doesn't know everything.

> One important caveat:
> Communication should be safe.

A Real Example: When A Good Plan Still Hurts

Alicia had a meticulously prepared estate plan and thought about every possibility. She named one daughter as her financial agent and trustee, and the other as her healthcare agent. She thought she was being fair and assumed that her daughters would appreciate her logic. Specifically, Alicia named one daughter as her financial agent because that daughter was more comfortable with finances, worked in the financial sector, was organized with paperwork, and was better suited to manage finances. Alicia named her other daughter as her healthcare agent because that daughter lived nearby, could get to the hospital quickly, and was more available to speak with doctors or make time-sensitive medical decisions. But Alicia never spoke with her daughters about her plan. Both daughters assumed the other had been favored, and the tension nearly unraveled the entire plan. The irony? They both agreed with the roles once they understood the reasoning behind Alicia's plan. But the delay in that understanding caused unnecessary conflict.

Setting Expectations Reduces Conflict

Communication is also your opportunity to set expectations. If you're leaving unequal inheritances, explain why. If you've decided to sell the family cabin instead of passing it on, share your reasons. If you're naming someone outside the family as your personal representative or trustee, tell your family why you believe that person is the best fit. You don't have to justify your choices—but explaining your concerns and why you made the decisions can prevent emotional fallout later. For example, "I'm naming Alex as trustee because she works in finance and is generally more detail-oriented—not because I value anyone more."

Discourage litigation. Persuade your neighbors to compromise whenever you can. Point out to them how the nominal winner is often a real loser in fees, expenses, and waste of time.

—Abraham Lincoln

When Less Is More

Talking about your estate plan isn't about getting everyone to agree. It's about helping them understand. Your plan is your own—but if you want it to succeed, your loved ones need to be able to carry it out without confusion or conflict.

In the next chapter, we'll look at the people you're relying on to help carry out your plan: your family, friends, and fiduciaries. The people you choose for your plan and how you prepare them can make all the difference.

Key Takeaways

Communication protects the plan.
Documents work better when people understand the roles and the why.

Silence creates conflict faster than honesty does.
Surprises breed suspicion, even when the plan is fair.

The goal is clarity, not consensus.
These conversations aren't about getting permission from your loved ones—they're about preventing confusion.

Communication should be safe and appropriate to the family.
In high-conflict situations, limited disclosure with professional guidance may be best.

Chapter 18

The Importance Of The Right People

Considering Professional Fiduciaries

Wisdom does not come overnight.
—African proverb

One of the most overlooked parts of estate planning isn't the documents—it's the people named to carry them out. A will, trust, or power of attorney can be drafted perfectly and still fall apart in real life if the wrong person is named as the personal representative, trustee, or agent. The roles in an estate plan aren't honorary titles. They are jobs—sometimes time-consuming, sometimes emotionally charged, and often unfamiliar to the people you ask to take on the responsibility.

Not every important person in a plan is a fiduciary making decisions for you, but it is worth considering having a team in place to make the difficult transitions a little easier. A *trusted contact* is someone who knows where the important documents and information are—think about your financial advisor, attorney, or accountant. They can help your appointed fiduciary get things done. A *fiduciary* is someone with legal authority and duties—such as a personal representative, trustee, or agent under a power of attorney. Most plans work best when both are present: someone with authority and someone with practical access and context.

Choosing who will carry out your wishes—whether as personal representative, trustee, power of attorney agent, or healthcare agent—is as critical as writing the plan itself.

This person or team of people will become your voice if you can no longer speak for yourself.

You trust these people to make the difficult decisions for you if you cannot. And too often, that responsibility is handed over without much discussion or thought.

> Choosing who will carry out your wishes is as critical as writing the plan itself.

Why "Closest" Isn't Always "Best"

Many clients I speak with begin their planning with a simple assumption: They'll name their spouse, their eldest child (or children in order from oldest to youngest), or the closest relative. Sometimes that works, but in many scenarios it doesn't. When it doesn't, the consequences can be difficult and even devastating.

Family dynamics are complicated. Geography, personal responsibility, interpersonal conflicts, or financial inexperience can all make even a well-meaning loved one a poor choice for the job. And that's where professional fiduciaries come into play.

What A Professional Fiduciary Is

Professional fiduciaries are individuals or institutions outside your circle of family or friends that you can appoint to handle your estate, trust, and financial matters. Professional fiduciaries come into the picture when neutrality, continuity, and competence matter most. They are particularly useful when there's conflict between beneficiaries, when assets are complex, when key decision-makers live far away, or when there simply isn't a reliable person available to carry the load.

Even in close families, naming a professional fiduciary as a successor can function as a safety net—quietly protecting the plan if life changes, health declines, or relationships shift.

If you do not have a will or plan for your estate, then the government has one for you.

—Shez Christopher

When A Professional Makes Sense

Choosing a professional fiduciary isn't shunning your family or close friends. It's a wise and proactive decision for people who want continuity, professionalism, and accountability in managing their estate or personal affairs. Sometimes it is appropriate for a couple with young children to name a professional fiduciary to manage their estate and finances if they prioritize continuity of financial care for their kids but cannot rely on a family member or friend to take on this role.

A fiduciary can serve as your personal representative (executor), trustee, agent under a power of attorney, or even court-appointed guardian or conservator. Unlike family members, who may be emotionally overwhelmed or unsure about their roles, professional fiduciaries are trained and experienced in managing estates, navigating legal requirements, and keeping clear records.

Cost, Compensation, And The Real Price Of Conflict

This is a common concern, but let's put it into perspective. Yes, a professional fiduciary charges for their services—but this is typically the case for anyone managing an estate. Even family members can (and often do) request compensation from the estate for their time and effort.

More importantly, the cost of mismanagement, delays, disputes, or court involvement can far exceed the cost of hiring a competent fiduciary from the start. I've seen families torn apart over disputes that could have been avoided with neutral administration.

Some clients choose a hybrid approach: Name a family member as co-trustee or co-agent alongside a professional or name a professional as a successor in case the primary person becomes unwilling or unable to serve. This gives families flexibility while still ensuring continuity.

How To Find The Right Professional

Start by asking your estate planning attorney for recommendations. Many trust companies offer fiduciary services or can direct you to vetted professionals who have experience handling estates like yours. That list gets bigger when you incorporate local agencies that provide specific fiduciary services—these are like a trust company but not tied to a specific bank or financial institution. Even so, local fiduciary agencies also focus on making financial (and sometimes medical) decisions for people who need someone to rely on outside of the circle of family and friends.

Your estate planning documents should clearly identify the fiduciary, spell out their powers, any limitations, and how they may be replaced if necessary.

How To Vet A Professional Fiduciary

When vetting a professional fiduciary, it helps to interview them the way one would interview any advisor: Ask about their experience and availability, how they onboard a new client, what roles they commonly serve in (trustee, agent, personal representative), how they communicate with family, what their fee structure looks like, what safeguards they use to prevent errors or misuse, whether they carry appropriate insurance, and how many people they currently serve.

It's not just about credentials—it's about fit and philosophy.

> It's not just about credentials—it's about fit and philosophy.

Bottom Line: Build A Plan That Is Pressure-Tested

Although many clients I have worked with tend to select close family or friends as their fiduciaries, it is important to know there are other options when family members or friends are not the best fit for the job. What matters in the end is how well our plans are put into action, and sometimes that means we don't give the people we love the full responsibility of all the difficult decisions. Ultimately, you know your loved ones best, and you are in the best position to decide if you can rely on them to take on the responsibility when the time comes.

Whether you rely on loved ones, professionals, or a combination of both, make those choices carefully. The right people can carry your plan forward with compassion, competence, and clarity. The wrong ones can derail even the best-laid plans.

Once the right people are identified—and the right backups are in place—the plan becomes that much stronger. It becomes a system that can function under stress. Next, we'll shift from who carries out the plan to examining a set of common pressure points that quietly derail even well-drafted plans if they aren't reviewed and coordinated.

Key Takeaways

Coordinating the right documents is only part of the challenge.
The people chosen to carry them out can determine whether the plan succeeds or unravels.

Default choices are not always the right choices.
Naming a family member may be most convenient, but competence, availability, and temperament matter more.

Professional fiduciaries add neutrality and continuity.
They can reduce conflict, handle complexity, and follow instructions without emotional entanglement.

Vetting is part of responsible planning.
Interviewing professional fiduciaries and understanding fees, processes, insurance, and communication style improves outcomes.

Chapter 19

Protecting Your Digital Assets

Vision without action is a daydream.
Action without vision is a nightmare.
—Japanese proverb

Think about how much of your modern life exists behind a login. Photos. Email. Bank accounts. Cryptocurrency. Cloud storage. Social media. Streaming subscriptions. Loyalty rewards. Even the notes app on your smartphone. The list grows every year.

If something happened to you tomorrow, would anyone know what digital accounts you have—or how to access them?

Digital assets aren't a single category. Some are financial. Some are contractual. Some are purely personal. But they share one important trait: Without clear authority and a workable plan, they can become inaccessible at the exact moment your loved ones need them.

The Problem: Access Is Not Automatic

Digital assets are often overlooked because they don't feel like estate planning property.

Unlike a filing cabinet or a safe deposit box, you can't simply hand someone the key to your digital assets.

Privacy laws, platform policies, and security features are designed to keep other people out—even family members, even the person named in a will—unless the right authority and verification are in place.

This gets even harder in the real world. Many accounts are "paperless" by default. Bills arrive by email. Statements live in online dashboards. Two-factor authentication is tied to a phone that no one can unlock. And once the original owner is gone—or incapacitated—families can lose weeks or months trying to piece together access that could have been made straightforward with preparation.

Perhaps you have already heard stories of people scrambling to access their cryptocurrency wallets or assets after forgetting their passwords.[55] Imagine how much worse it would be for loved ones having to figure this out for you.

> Unlike a filing cabinet or a safe deposit box, you can't simply hand someone the key to your digital assets.

The Law Controls Who Gets In

The Revised Uniform Fiduciary Access to Digital Assets Act (RUFADAA) has been adopted by many US states, including Colorado,[56] and allows individuals to legally authorize their fiduciaries to access digital assets. Under laws like RUFADAA, access often depends on the instructions left in the platform's settings, the estate planning documents, and the provider's process. In many cases, the platform's built-in "legacy tool"—if used—can control how access is handled, which is why coordination matters.

Access isn't automatic just because someone has a title. In many cases, the outcome depends on three moving parts working together: (1) the platform's own settings (including any legacy tool you activated), (2) the specific authority granted in your estate planning documents, and (3) the provider's verification process. When those parts align, access can be manageable. When they don't, families can find themselves locked out—sometimes permanently.

Where To Start

It can feel intimidating at first, but it doesn't have to be. The best first step is to create a secure, updated inventory of your digital accounts—anything that holds money, carries legal significance, or contains personal information your loved ones may need. That includes email, online banking, and investment accounts, social media, cloud storage, cryptocurrency wallets or exchanges, subscription services, loyalty accounts, and any domain names or websites you own.

A password manager can make this much easier, but one rule matters: Don't place passwords or login details in your will or estate planning documents. Those documents are not designed to store sensitive access information, and they may become accessible to others after death or during administration. Instead, keep your inventory in a secure location (digital or physical), and in your estate plan, simply reference where it is stored and who has authority to access it.

Even a basic written list kept somewhere safe is better than nothing—so long as it's protected, updated periodically, and your personal representative or designated agent knows how to find it. If a secure digital vault or document storage service fits your style, that can be an excellent option, and I'll cover practical storage strategies in the next chapter.

Build Legal Authority Into Your Core Documents

An inventory helps someone know what exists. Legal authority helps them take action. Consider working with your estate planning attorney to ensure your documents grant legal authority over digital assets during incapacity and after death. This should be done through a durable power of attorney and trust for periods of incapacity, and in your will and/or trust for after death. Even though many states grant the personal representative (or executor) specific access, it doesn't hurt to ensure you specifically grant your personal representative authority over digital assets in your estate planning documents.

Platform Tools Help—But They Don't Replace Planning

Beyond legal paperwork, some major tech companies now offer digital legacy tools that let you grant someone access or control after your death. Google has an Inactive Account Manager[57] that lets you choose a trusted person to access your Google account if it becomes inactive. Facebook lets you appoint a Legacy Contact who can manage your memorialized Facebook profile.[58] Apple's Digital Legacy[59] feature lets you designate individuals to access your Apple ID and associated data in your account. Instagram,[60] LinkedIn,[61] and X[62] (formerly known as Twitter) all offer forms to request account removal or memorialization.

Password managers can also be helpful here, especially those that offer an "emergency access" or legacy feature—but the goal is secure transfer, not sharing passwords casually.

These tools can be useful, but they don't solve the entire problem. They don't always allow access to all content, and they vary widely in terms of what they require and allow. Careful estate planning remains essential.

If you don't design your own life plan,
chances are you'll fall into someone else's plan.
And guess what they have planned for you?
Not much.
—Jim Rohn

The Locked Laptop

Kevin came to me for help managing the estate of his brother, Liam, after Liam passed away unexpectedly. Kevin and Liam lived in different states. Although Liam was organized in many areas of his life, before he passed away, he didn't write down any digital logins, passwords, or account information.

Liam's entire financial life—from online banking to investment accounts to bill paying was managed electronically, and there wasn't a recent paper bill or invoice to be found in his home. Both Liam's computer and his smartphone were locked and password-protected, but nobody knew his passwords. It took months of legal back-and-forth and costly IT services to even achieve partial access to Liam's digital life. Some accounts were never recovered.

The family did everything right after the fact, but that still could not undo the stress or the knowledge that a portion of Liam's estate was now permanently lost to his family. In the digital age, the keys to the digital aspects of your estate aren't in a file cabinet. They're behind logins, two-factor authentication, and encrypted devices.

A Quick Note On Electronic Estate Planning Documents

In recent years, several states have passed laws that permit the creation of entirely electronic wills that never need to be printed. According to Trust & Will, as of July 2023, fourteen states plus the District of Columbia and the US Virgin Islands now allow testators to execute wills electronically.[63] That shift is a strong indicator that more states will follow. Electronic estate planning documents are available in some states, and the number of states that allow them is likely to increase.[64] They are in their infancy, and there are many legal and logistical hurdles that the legal community needs to cross before widespread use.

In response to the constraints of the COVID-19 pandemic, many states moved quickly to authorize remote notarization for legal documents.[65] As of 2024, forty-seven states and the District of Columbia authorize remote notarization for legal documents. As a result, a growing number now also allow virtual witnessing, helping make digital execution and storage of estate documents more widely available.

Of course, this shift opens a whole new can of worms—from questions about authentication and fraud prevention to major variations in how states handle digital estate documents. It's a fascinating and evolving area, one that arguably deserves an entire book of its own. For the purpose of this book, the takeaway is simple: Going digital can be practical, but it must be done correctly and in compliance with the laws of the state that will govern your documents.

Digital assets are no longer optional for most of us.

They're part of modern life—and they deserve the same planning attention as our physical possessions.

> Digital assets are no longer optional for most of us.

Looking Ahead

Creating a plan is one thing. Making sure your loved ones can find it—and use it—is another. A large number of personal representatives don't even know they've been named in someone's will—let alone where to find the documents.[66] In the next chapter, we'll focus on practical, secure ways to store your estate planning documents (physical and digital) and how to make your plan discoverable and accessible when it matters most.

Key Takeaways

Digital assets are part of modern estate planning.
Online accounts can hold money, legal rights, and irreplaceable personal information.

Access is not automatic.
Loved ones may be locked out without clear legal authority and proper verification.

An inventory is the first step.
A secure, updated list helps fiduciaries know what exists and where to look.

Passwords do not belong in estate planning documents.
Instead, the plan should reference where access information is stored and who can reach it.

Platform "legacy tools" can help, but they are not a full solution.
They vary widely and should support—not replace—coordinated legal planning.

Discoverability matters.
A plan that can't be found or accessed when needed is a plan that can't work.

Chapter 20

Where Your Plan Lives

Secure Document Storage And Access

An hour of planning can save you ten hours of doing.
—Dale Carnegie

Now that we have walked through the components of the estate plan, you are ready to make careful decisions and sign your plan into action. Keep in mind that an estate plan isn't truly ready until the right people can locate it and use it. Your fiduciaries need more than legal authority—they need a clear path to the documents and the information that tells them what exists, where it's held, and what to do next.

In practice, your loved ones need two things: (1) the plan itself, and (2) a practical road map that helps them identify your major accounts, assets, and key contacts without forcing your trusted decision-makers to play detective.

Finding Your Plan Matters

Let's say you have made the tough decisions, executed your estate planning documents, and created a plan that protects your legacy and your loved ones. Stopping here can complicate matters for the trusted decision-makers in your plan. Even the most carefully crafted estate plan is not going to be useful to anyone if it is buried in a stack of paperwork.

But beyond that, our estate plan provides guidance on what to do if we become incapacitated or pass away; it doesn't include information on where all the accounts are and how to get into them. In practice, I learned that unraveling this part is just as big a hurdle for our loved ones, if not bigger than, figuring out the estate plan itself. Knowing where your plan lives, along with a blueprint to understand and access your major assets—both physically and digitally—matters just as much as what the plan says.

Not leaving a clear road map for loved ones is an all-too-common issue.

Many estate plans fall apart because no one can find the legal documents or has any idea where the major accounts are held. In some difficult cases, personal representatives are forced to start looking for accounts or safe deposit boxes at nearby banks. Sometimes they have to go back to their loved one's former employer to ask for additional financial records, or even request copies of their loved one's credit reports. All of this happens because their loved one left no road map to follow.

> Not leaving a clear road map for loved ones is an all-too-common issue.

The Paperwork Nightmare

Both of Mike's parents passed away, one shortly after the other. Mike, who was the oldest child, stepped in to handle everything. He, like his siblings, was grieving the loss of his parents and was now also the one responsible for sorting through the legal and financial details of his parents' estate. He wanted to do the right thing. He wanted to handle the estate in a way that would make his parents proud.

But instead of having a clear plan to follow, he was left to piece things together on his own. Piece by piece, he began finding documents, but they did not tell the whole story. Old bank statements. Insurance documents. Unopened mail. Outdated files. It was a lot for Mike to process. Some documents were current. Some were years out of date.

Mike had helped his parents over the years and thought that he had a pretty good idea of what they owned. But the more he looked, the more he realized he did not have the full picture. He found paperwork for another bank account. Then another life insurance policy. Mail started arriving from financial institutions he didn't recognize. And just when he thought he was making progress, another document, account, or question would appear. Some accounts had beneficiaries listed. Some didn't. Some accounts could be transferred directly. Others had to go through probate.

There is no magic wand we can wave to correct the lack of proper planning. What we can do is bring order to the process, one step at a time. Together with Mike, we built a road map and had to contact financial institutions one by one to identify any additional accounts that were missing. We figured out the hard way what accounts were current and what information was outdated.

The complicated process added to Mike's pain, and it was not easy or quick. It took over two years before we were able to finish the entire probate process, and we hit some bumps along the way. I remember him saying that he wouldn't wish this "scavenger hunt" on anyone. At the end, Mike said to me:

"I wish I talked to you sooner. You could have helped us avoid this whole mess."

Unfortunately, this story is all too familiar to me because I regularly help clients in similar situations. Even when we take the time to craft an estate plan for our loved ones to follow, we often overlook the logistics of providing access and important information to our trusted agents. Storing your estate plan securely—while still making it accessible to the right people—is an essential part of finishing the planning process. Here's how some people are doing it today.

> "I wish I talked to you sooner. You could have helped us avoid this whole mess."

Physical Storage Options

Some clients choose traditional methods, such as storing original documents in a home safe, a fireproof box, or a locked, fireproof filing cabinet. I typically recommend a fireproof box or safe to my clients, as long as the right people in their lives have access to it and know what to expect to find inside. This approach works well when a trusted family member or personal representative knows the location and the combination or key is accessible.

Some people leave original estate planning documents with their attorney. However, many attorneys have moved away from holding onto original client documents for various reasons.

For people looking for more traditional, physical storage options, you can explore Nokbox or CLEAR Kits, which offer a platform to help you create an organized "next of kin" plan. This provides an organizational system for multiple items, such as estate documents, passwords, bill information, account instructions, and more, in what is essentially a tabbed, organized case. These are designed for those who would like to keep and store paper documents in an organized manner to ease the transition for their loved ones.

The Safe Deposit Box: "Safe" Can Sometimes Become "Sealed Off"

This brings me to another cautionary tale about using a bank safe deposit box to store an estate plan or other important documents. Sam's father had a well-drafted will, but he tucked it away in a safe deposit box. His father decided to use a nearby bank that was not his primary bank. He never told anyone where it was and didn't give a spare key to any of his family members.

When Sam's father passed away, the family didn't even know which branch of this large bank the safe deposit box was in. There were also no records of this safe deposit box to be found at his home. The only reason the family knew they should be looking was that their father proudly explained he had signed a will and put it "somewhere safe."

After a frustrating scavenger hunt involving asking multiple banks, they finally located the box—only to learn it would require a locksmith to drill it open because they couldn't find the key. Ironically, if the family hadn't known Dad left a will, they would have never even considered searching for it, and their father's estate would have been probated through the default state intestacy rules. All this trouble the family went through just to get access to a document that should have been ready and accessible in a moment of need.

Searching for a will is not a rare experience for families. If you are considering using a safe deposit box, make sure your decision-maker knows where it is and has access. This type of issue can and should be avoided.

Digital Vaults And Online Storage Tools

To address the lack of access and disorganization, some are turning to digital tools. These services can help people securely store documents online and provide trusted individuals with access either immediately or after death. To solve the access problem, some people use secure digital vaults designed for end-of-life and incapacity organization.

For example, My Life & Wishes[67] allows users to store estate planning documents and organize key account information in one place, then share access with trusted contacts. Other platforms take a similar approach, with different features and price points. The best system is the one you'll actually keep updated—and that your fiduciaries can realistically use when the moment comes.

Another option is a service called DocuBank.[68] DocuBank stores advance directives and medical powers of attorney, providing emergency access to hospitals and healthcare providers.

Everplans[69] provides a similar digital vault approach, with the added feature of granting different levels of access to different people, so your financial advisor doesn't have to see your funeral playlist unless you want them to.

Some estate planning attorneys and financial advisors offer clients access to proprietary or subscription-based digital storage portals as part of their services. FidSafe,[70] by Fidelity, is one such option. These tools often allow secure uploading and sharing of your plan, keeping everything in one place and accessible to your designated contacts.

This is by no means an exhaustive list. Other digital storage and estate organization services include Trustworthy,[71] LifeSite,[72] and GoodTrust.[73] Each offers a slightly different focus—from digital legacy planning to healthcare preferences and document vaults. Depending on your needs, budget, and comfort level with technology, one or more of these tools may be a fit.

The downside of some of these tools is that they encourage people to fill out their own plans using their software—a practice that I would strongly discourage for most people. The next chapter is dedicated to this topic.

Choosing A System That Will Actually Work For You

When choosing where to store your documents, it's important to think about longevity and ease of use. Will your personal representative or trustee be able to log in if you're gone? Will they need a password or key you haven't shared? Will they need to look for the documents in your home, or would you prefer to provide digital copies? Does the platform have customer service if something goes wrong?

In my practice, I've seen clients benefit from using a structured digital vault system because it reduces the scavenger-hunt problem and keeps everything organized in one place. I use My Life & Wishes in my practice because I've seen firsthand the importance of helping clients stay organized.

I'm not a fan of having clients make paper copies of their estate planning documents and handing them out to loved ones. From experience, I recognize that paper copies are often not up-to-date and tend to get misplaced. Rather than having clients rely only on paper copies, I provide a practical digital resource that is easier to update and manage. Plus, I find that this provides the additional encouragement clients need to take the steps to leave an organized road map for their loved ones.

What makes greatness is starting something
that lives after you.
—Ralph W. Sockman

Make Your Plan Actionable

As we continue forward, we'll take a deeper look at organizing your digital and physical assets, tracking key accounts, and building a checklist your loved ones can follow. Because having a plan is only the first step. Making it actionable is just as important as the plan itself.

Whatever storage method you choose, the key is not just to protect the documents—it's to make sure someone you trust knows where they are and how to access them. So go ahead and *tell* them. Better yet, walk them through it.

Here's the reality: The best estate plan isn't the most expensive one, or the most complicated one. It's the one that actually works when it's needed. And that depends heavily on how it was created. In the next chapter, we'll take an honest look at DIY estate planning versus professional planning—what online tools do well, where they tend to break down, and the situations where hiring help isn't a luxury, it's practical.

Key Takeaways

An estate plan must be accessible to work.
A perfectly drafted plan can still fail if no one can find it or use it in real time.

Your fiduciaries need a road map, not just documents.
They must know what exists, where it is held, and how to begin—without acting as a detective.

Safe storage should be accessible.
If originals are locked away without clear access, families can lose valuable time when decisions are urgent.

Digital storage can help you get organized.
The best system is the one trusted people can actually access.

Finishing the plan means planning for the handoff.
A plan isn't complete at signing—it's complete when the right people are ready to take over.

Chapter 21

DIY Or Professional? Choosing The Right Path For Your Estate Plan

The best way to predict the future is to create it.
—Often attributed to Peter Drucker

Every week, someone asks me, "Do I really need an attorney for this, or can I just use something online?" It's a fair question. Many people view wills and trusts as a commodity, thinking they are all the same, and decide the best deal they can get is what they will use. With platforms like LegalZoom, Rocket Lawyer, and Trust & Will offering fast, low-cost options, the DIY route can feel like the practical answer, especially when money is tight. Some people believe online plan preparation is best for them simply because it could save them money and help them avoid thinking about alternatives.

Remember that there is no one-size-fits-all approach to planning.

This chapter isn't here to shame anyone for choosing a DIY option. But it is here to make one thing clear: There's a difference between generating documents and building a plan that actually works when it's needed. The right choice depends on what you're trying to accomplish—and what risks you're willing to accept.

As with any unfamiliar professional service, estate planning is easier to navigate when you have guidance. An experienced attorney understands the process, legal requirements, risks, and details that are easy for a layperson to miss. Would you sell your house without a real estate professional? Some people do, but they should go into the process accepting that there may be bumps in the road and that they may not end up with the best deal. If you are not as knowledgeable as a real estate professional, you may miss things that end up costing you (or your estate) money and time.

> Remember that there is no one-size-fits-all approach to planning.

What DIY Tools Do

Online estate planning tools are popular for a reason. They're convenient, they're quick, and they tend to be the most affordable option. They can also serve as a meaningful entry point for people who would otherwise do nothing at all. And for someone with very simple assets, no dependents, no complex family dynamics, and a realistic understanding of the limitations, DIY documents may be better than having a wish and a prayer that things go smoothly.

DIY tools can be especially helpful in time-sensitive situations—when someone needs something in place immediately, and professional help isn't available fast enough. In that sense, DIY planning can function as a temporary bridge.

What DIY Tools Don't Do

The limitation is straightforward: Online services generate documents. They do not provide legal advice, inform you about blind spots, or help you coordinate the moving parts of your plan.

They typically won't walk you through how beneficiary designations interact with a will, how titling affects probate, whether a trust is appropriate (or how to fund it), or how to reduce the likelihood of conflict in a blended family. They don't follow up, and they don't know what you *mean* if some of your form answers are ambiguous. They fill in templates based on what you type into the form—nothing more and nothing less.

And even a well-written document can fail if it isn't executed correctly. Execution formality rules vary by state. Witnessing, notarization, and signing formalities matter. When people miss those steps—or assume the document is valid because it was printed from a reputable website—the plan breaks down at the exact moment it's supposed to protect the family.

I've also reviewed DIY documents where the language was vague or inconsistent, creating more confusion than clarity. I have seen DIY documents that were not properly signed and completed. In those situations, the person using the online services thought they were doing the right thing. But good intentions can only get us so far if instructions don't translate cleanly into action.

For every complex problem there is an answer that is clear, simple, and wrong.

—H. L. Mencken

When Professional Planning Is Worth It

Working with an estate planning attorney isn't about simply paying someone else to draft forms for you. It's paying for guidance, strategy, and coordination—so the plan reflects your real-life situation.

A skilled attorney helps identify issues that people don't know to look for, including inconsistencies between documents and accounts, conflicts in fiduciary roles, tax or creditor concerns, and planning pitfalls unique to second marriages, minor children, or family conflict. A good attorney will also ensure the documents are properly executed, legally enforceable, and aligned with the assets they are intended to control. If a trust is part of the plan, professional planning typically includes clear instructions for funding and maintaining it—because an unfunded trust is not worth the paper it is printed on.

Just as important, attorneys are accountable for their work and bound by professional and ethical obligations. A client isn't buying paperwork—they're buying a professional standard of care.

Cost: What You're Really Paying For

Yes, an attorney will usually cost more than a DIY service. But what you're paying for is experience, customization, coordination, and confidence that the plan is built to function in the real world.

A DIY plan can be cheap up front—and become much more expensive later if it triggers probate problems, court involvement, delays, or disputes. The short-term savings can easily turn into long-term costs paid by the estate, the beneficiaries, or both. As I often tell clients, they're not paying for documents. They're paying for peace of mind—and the reduced likelihood that their family will have to clean up preventable problems.

The DIY Trust: When Templates Create Work After Death

Naomi's mother downloaded a will and trust templates online and repurposed the documents for her and her blended family. The trust was signed but never funded. The will named one person as personal representative and distributed assets in one way. The trust named a different person as trustee and listed a different set of beneficiaries. The result was a mess: Much of the estate still had to go through probate, and the trust didn't meaningfully control anything until assets were eventually transferred into it through the probate process.

The adult children weren't just grieving—they were confused and upset because the process was taking much longer and involved much more work than they expected. Instead of a streamlined administration, the work was doubled.

It was a plan built without coordination, and it failed in the places that mattered most.

> It was a plan built without coordination, and it failed in the places that mattered most.

How To Choose The Right Attorney

If you decide to work with an attorney, it's worth finding someone who focuses on estate planning and understands situations like yours. Not all attorneys are the same, and estate planning is one of those areas where experience and process matter.

Here are some questions you can ask prospective attorneys as you're deciding who to work with:

- How much of your practice is dedicated to estate planning?

- Do you regularly work with clients in my situation (blended families, small business owners, aging parents, etc.)?
- Do you draft both wills and trusts, and help clients decide which type of plan is a better fit for them?
- Do you charge flat fees or hourly? What's included?
- If a trust is part of the plan, will you provide funding guidance and beneficiary coordination?
- How do future updates work?
- Do you offer digital document storage guidance?
- Do you work with professional fiduciaries?
- Do you have a succession plan if you retire or become unavailable?
- If my family needs help with administration later, can you assist?

These aren't just nice-to-know questions. They help ensure you're hiring someone who will build a plan that works for you and give you peace of mind.

Final Thoughts

Ultimately, the right path—DIY or professional—depends on your goals, your life, and your circumstances. For some people, a reputable DIY tool can be a meaningful first step. For many others, especially when families are blended, assets are significant, or emotions are complicated, professional planning is less about just getting the plan in place and more about protection.

What matters most is this: Your plan should work in the real world, under stress, when you're not available to explain what you meant and where to start. It should be clear, consistent, properly executed, and easy for the people you've chosen to carry out.

If reading this book has done anything, I hope it has replaced uncertainty with momentum and answered some of your questions. You don't need to do everything at once—but you do need to start, and you need to start with intention. In the epilogue, I'll point you to practical, free resources I've created to help you take the next step.

Key Takeaways

A DIY plan can be a better-than-nothing starting point.
But you should be aware of the limitations associated with DIY planning.

Online platforms generate documents; they do not provide legal guidance.
They don't coordinate assets, beneficiaries, or real-world logistics.

Mistakes can break the plan.
Signing formalities, vague language, and unfunded trusts create costly messes.

Professional planning is about strategy and coordination.
A good attorney aligns your documents with your assets and your family dynamics.

The goal isn't paperwork—it's peace of mind.
Choose the path that creates a plan your loved ones can actually use.

Epilogue

Where To Go From Here

You've made it to the end of the book! Thank you for taking the time to read this book and for arming yourself with the information I hope will be of good use. You've learned what the tools are, how they work, and where estate plans commonly break down. That puts you ahead of the game—because the biggest risk in estate planning is doing nothing and hoping things will work out anyway. I hope you will use what you learned and share it with others.

I wrote this book to offer practical guidance and to educate people about an often-misunderstood topic. In that spirit, I want to challenge you to take the next step with your estate planning journey. Turn your newfound motivation into an actionable plan—something you and your loved ones can use. That means organizing key information, reducing guesswork, and making your wishes easy to find.

To help with that, I maintain a free resource library on my website. It's designed to be a source of quick guides, checklists, and helpful tools you can use whether you're building a plan now, reviewing your existing plan, or managing someone's estate after they passed away.

> Check out my free resource library:
> https://premierlegacylaw.com/resources/

If You're Starting From Scratch

Begin with my Estate Planning Preparedness Checklist. It helps you gather the information that makes planning faster, less expensive, and more accurate, so you're not trying to remember everything in the middle of an appointment or a crisis.

If You Already Have Some Documents But Want To Improve The Plan

Review the Top 5 Estate Planning Mistakes to Avoid and the guide on how an estate works with a will and a trust. These are designed to help you spot the gaps that cause the most trouble—like outdated beneficiary designations, missing fiduciary conversations, and documents that exist on paper but aren't actually usable.

If You Want Your Plan To Be Accessible In The Real World

Take a look at my materials on document organization and secure storage, including information about the Legacy Vault. A plan that can't be found—or can't be accessed—isn't a plan. It's a file.

If You're Dealing With Probate Or Trust Administration Right Now

Start with the Survivor's Guide, the Basics of the Probate Process, and the Successor Trustee's Initial Checklist. These resources are built to reduce overwhelm and give you a clear, steady first set of steps.

No matter where you are in the process, the goal is the same: Make life easier for the people you love. If you take one action after finishing this book, let it be this: Choose a starting point, download the resource that fits your situation, and take the next step.

Your loved ones and the future you will be grateful you did.

APPENDICES

Appendix A

Questions To Ask Yourself To Jumpstart Your Estate Planning

If you're not sure where to begin, these questions can help you clarify what matters most. You don't need all the answers today—but asking the right questions is the first step toward a solid, personalized plan.

Personal And Family

- Who depends on me—financially, emotionally, or physically?
- Who do I trust to make decisions for me if I can't speak for myself?
- Have I talked to the people I would name in my plan?
- Are there any family dynamics that could complicate things if I don't plan?

Health And Incapacity

- If I became seriously ill or injured, who should make medical decisions for me?
- What kind of care would I want—or not want—in a medical emergency?

- Have I documented my preferences in a healthcare directive or living will?
- Who will be best suited to make difficult medical decisions for me and honor my wishes?

Finances And Property

- Who should manage my finances if I become incapacitated?
- Are my assets organized in a way that someone else could step in and manage them?
- Do I know which accounts or policies require a named beneficiary?
- Have I updated my beneficiary designations recently?

Legacy And Distribution

- Who should receive my property or assets when I die?
- Are there specific items I want to leave to certain people?
- Are there charities, causes, or organizations I'd like to support?
- Do I want to put restrictions or conditions on how someone receives their inheritance?

Children And Dependents

- Who should take care of my minor children if I'm no longer able?
- Have I named a guardian in my estate plan?
- Do I have a plan to support children or other dependents financially?

Digital And Practical Details

- Does someone know how to access my digital accounts (email, bank, social media)?
- Did I prepare and update a list of major accounts, policies, and assets that my agents will need access to if something goes wrong?
- Do I use a password manager—and is anyone set up to access it?
- Have I told anyone where my estate planning documents are stored?

Appendix B

Acknowledgments

This book exists because a lot of people carried me—sometimes quietly, sometimes loudly, and other times when I didn't even realize I needed it.

First, to my wonderful wife, Vanya: Thank you for being my rock and greatest cheerleader. You believed in this project from the beginning and believed in me. Thank you for the many conversations, the ideas, the honest feedback, the patience, and the steady encouragement that kept me moving when the finish line felt far away. You helped me sharpen my ideas and stay grounded in why this work matters.

To my sister, Michelle: Thank you for being a sounding board, test subject, and a source of perspective. Your support gave me clarity, and your tenacity continues to inspire me.

To Mimi and Nick: Thank you for your kindness, encouragement, and support. I'm grateful for your generosity and the many ways you have helped and cared for our family.

To all my family and friends: Thank you for supporting me and offering steady encouragement.

To Henry DeVries: Thank you for helping me shape this book into something clearer, stronger, and more readable—without losing my voice. And to the team at Indie Books International, thank you for guiding me through a publishing process I started without knowing the first thing about how it works.

To my former colleagues and coworkers: Thank you for your mentorship, your guiding hand, and the lessons that helped form the foundation of my professional life.

To the multiple other mentors who helped along the way: Thank you for your patience, your guidance, and your steady commitment to doing difficult work in the justice system the right way.

And to my clients: Thank you for trusting me during some of the most difficult moments of your lives. Your courage, your questions, and your stories shaped how I practice law and how I think about estate planning. You reminded me again and again why I do this job every day. I'm honored to have been invited into your lives, and I hope this book reflects what you taught me.

Finally, thank you to every reader who picks up this book. If it helps you feel more prepared, more confident, or simply less lost in the process, then it was all worthwhile.

Appendix C

About The Author

Ilya Lyubimskiy, JD, CPA, is the founder and managing attorney of Premier Legacy Law, an estate planning and probate law firm that focuses on helping clients with estate planning, probate, and trust administration.

In addition to his estate planning and probate experience, Ilya's legal background includes serving as a prosecutor, where he advocated for victims of financial crime—work that inspired his passion for helping people protect their legacies and families.

Ilya grew up in Colorado. He earned his law degree from the University of Denver Sturm College of Law and his Bachelor of Science in Accounting from Metropolitan State University of Denver. He is also a licensed Certified Public Accountant in Colorado.

A core part of Ilya's work is education. He is passionate about empowering people with the knowledge and resources they need to make informed legacy planning and estate administration decisions. He regularly educates both members of the public and other professionals on various legal topics within the legacy planning and estate administration realms. Ilya feels fulfilled when empowering people with the tools and knowledge they need to safeguard their legacies and families.

Ilya lives in the Denver metropolitan area with his wife and their dog, Sammy.

More information is available at https://premierlegacylaw.com.

Appendix D

Works Cited And Author's Notes

1 Victoria Lurie, "2025 Wills and Estate Planning Study," Caring.com, updated February 11, 2026, https://www.caring.com/resources/wills-survey/.

2 Lurie, "2025 Wills and Estate Planning Study."

3 John Walsh, Michael Neal, and Amalie Zinn, "Prospective Heirs' Property Among Older Homeowners," *Urban Institute*, October 30, 2024, https://www.urban.org/research/publication/prospective-heirs-property-among-older-homeowners.

4 George Michelsen Foy, "Humans Can't Plan Long-Term, and Here's Why," Psychology Today (blog), May 12, 2025, https://www.psychologytoday.com/us/blog/shut-up-and-listen/201806/humans-cant-plan-long-term-and-heres-why.

5 Jilenne Gunther, "The Scope of Elder Financial Exploitation: What It Costs Victims," AARP, June 2023, https://www.aarp.org/content/dam/aarp/money/scams-and-fraud/2023/true-cost-elder-financial-exploitation.doi.10.26419-2Fppi.00194.001.pdf.

6 "Get the Facts on Elder Abuse," National Council on Aging, July 08, 2024, https://www.ncoa.org/article/get-the-facts-on-elder-abuse/.

7 "The Top 5 Financial Scams Targeting Older Adults," National Council on Aging, March 17, 2026, https://www.ncoa.org/article/top-5-financial-scams-targeting-older-adults.

8 "Taxpayers Beware: Tax Season Is Prime Time for Phone Scams," US Internal Revenue Service, January 27, 2022, https://www.irs.gov/newsroom/taxpayers-beware-tax-season-is-prime-time-for-phone-scams.

9 *2023 Elder Fraud Report,* Federal Bureau of Investigation, April 30, 2024, https://www.ic3.gov/annualreport/reports/2023_ic3elderfraudreport.pdf.

10 "Consumer Sentinel Network Data Book 2023," and "Press Release: Top Fraud," Federal Trade Commission, February 2024, https://www.ftc.gov/reports/consumer-sentinel-network-data-book-2023; and "FTC Takes Aim at Driving Losses Among Older Americans," Federal Trade Commission (news release), November 24, 2024, https://www.ftc.gov/news-events/news/press-releases/2024/11/ftc-takes-aim-top-fraud-driving-losses-among-older-americans.

11 "Will(ful) Neglect: Survey Reveals Nearly 60 percent of Americans Unprepared for the Inevitable," LegalShield, August 8, 2023, https://www.legalshield.com/newsroom/willful-neglect-survey-reveals-nearly-60-of-americans-unprepared-for-the-inevitable.

12 Rachel Lustbader, "2024 Wills and Estate Planning Study," Caring, The Free Senior Living Advisors, February 11, 2024, https://www.caring.com/resources/2024-wills-survey.

13 Sarah Jones, "Estate Planning Statistics to Read Before Writing Your Will," Legal Zoom, updated February 14, 2026, https://www.legalzoom.com/articles/estate-planning-statistics.

14 Bridging the Gap: The Importance of Estate Planning Through Generations, Cambridge Trust, Feb. 16, 2022, formerly available at https://www.cambridgetrust.com/CT/media/CTMedia/Images/Insights/Insight_graphics/Q1-Client-Update-2022-Bridging-the-Gap.pdf (link no longer active).

15 Jones, "Estate Planning Statistics."

16 Tali Sharot, *The Optimism Bias: A Tour of the Irrationally Positive Brain,* (Vintage Books, 2011).

17 Rachel Lustbader, "2023 Wills and Estate Planning Study," Caring.com, updated January 9, 2026, https://www.caring.com/resources/2023-wills-survey.

18 Jones, "Estate Planning Statistics."

19 Lurie, "2025 Wills and Estate Planning Study."
20 "Avoidance Behavior," *APA Dictionary of Psychology*, American Psychological Association, 2024, https://dictionary.apa.org/avoidance-behavior.
21 Rachel Lustbader, "2022 Study: The Effect of COVID-19 on Estate Planning," Caring.com, updated February 11, 2026, https://www.caring.com/resources/estate-planning-covid-19.
22 Lurie, "2025 Wills and Estate Planning Study."
23 Jones, "Estate Planning Statistics."
24 Lurie, "2025 Wills and Estate Planning Study."
25 "Bridging the Gap: The Importance of Estate Planning Through Generations," Cambridge Trust (Feb. 16, 2022), formerly available at: https://www.cambridgetrust.com/CT/media/CTMedia/Images/Insights/Insight_graphics/Q1-Client-Update-2022-Bridging-the-Gap.pdf (link no longer active).
26 Lisa Respers France, "Aretha Franklin's family heads to court in estate battle." CNN, July 10, 2023, https://www.cnn.com/2023/07/10/entertainment/aretha-franklin-wills-court/index.html.
27 Jones, "Estate Planning Statistics."
28 Suzanne Woolley, "Americans Don't Want to Talk About Generational Wealth," Bloomberg, April 6, 2022, https://www.bloomberg.com/news/articles/2022-04-06/americans-don-t-want-to-talk-about-their-generational-wealth.
29 Jonathan Spiteri and Philip von Brockdorff, "Household Wealth and Inheritance Transfers: Evidence from the Euro Area," *Journal of Family and Economic Issues* (2022), 1–15, doi:10.1007/s10834–022-09861-0.
30 Jones, "Estate Planning Statistics."
31 National Association of REALTORS®, "NAR Existing-Home Sales Report Shows 0.8% Increase in May," June 23, 2025, https://www.nar.realtor/newsroom/nar-existing-home-sales-report-shows-0-8-increase-in-may.
32 LegalShield, "Will(ful) Neglect."
33 Lustbader, "2024 Wills and Estate Planning Study."
34 See *Colorado Revised Statutes*, §15-11-101 et seq., "Intestate Estate," Colorado General Assembly, 2024.

35 Lurie, "2025 Wills and Estate Planning Study."

36 D. Johnston, "Succession," *The Cambridge Companion to Roman Law*, (Cambridge University Press, 2015), 199–212.

37 "Executive Branch Financial Disclosure, Qualified Trusts, and Certificates of Divestiture; Financial Disclosure Requirements for Interests in Revocable Inter Vivos Trusts," Federal Register, May 31, 2002, https://www.federalregister.gov/documents/2002/05/31/02-13734/executive-branch-financial-disclosure-qualified-trusts-and-certificates-of-divestiture-financial.

38 Maya Powers, "2025 Estate Planning Report," Trust & Will, April 27, 2026, https://trustandwill.com/learn/estate-planning-report-2025.

39 Jane Bryant Quinn, "Jane Bryant Quinn Explains the Role of Living Trusts," *AARP*, July 19, 2022, https://www.aarp.org/money/retirement/living-trust-uses/.

40 "Leaving a Legacy: A Lasting Gift to Loved Ones," Age Wave, accessed April 30, 2026, https://agewave.com/what-we-do/landmark-research-and-consulting/research-studies/leaving-a-legacy-a-lasting-gift-to-loved-ones/.

41 "Older Adults' Experiences with Advance Care Planning," National Poll on Healthy Aging, University of Michigan Institute for Healthcare Policy and Innovation, April 6, 2021, https://ihpi.umich.edu/national-poll-healthy-aging/national-findings/older-adults-experiences-advance-care-planning.

42 "Aging with Dignity", Five Wishes Program, accessed May 9, 2026, https://agingwithdignity.org/five-wishes/.

43 "Colorado MOST Medical Orders for Scope of Treatment", University of Colorado Anschutz, accessed May 9, 2026, https://www.cuanschutz.edu/centers/bioethicshumanities/comost.

44 National POLST Coalition, "Learn What a POLST Form Is, Who It's For, and How it Helps," accessed May 9, 2026, https://polst.org/for-patients/about-polst-form/.

45 Charles Sabatino, "Myths and Facts About Health Care Advance Directives," American Bar Association, October 1, 2015, https://www.americanbar.org/groups/law_aging/publications/bifocal/vol_37/issue_1_october2015/myths_and_facts_advance_directives/.

46 US Department of Health and Human Services, "HIPAA For Professionals," accessed May 9, 2026, https://www.hhs.gov/hipaa/for-professionals/index.html.

47 C. Christopher Hook and Paul S. Mueller, "The Terri Schiavo Saga: The Making of a Tragedy and Lessons Learned," *Mayo Clinic Proceedings* 80, no. 11, 1449–60, November 2005, https://www.mayoclinicproceedings.org/article/S0025-6196(11)61439-0/fulltext.

48 Weijer C. A death in the family: reflections on the Terri Schiavo case. CMAJ. 2005 Apr 26;172(9):1197-8. doi: 10.1503/cmaj.050348. Epub 2005 Apr 1. PMID: 15805148; PMCID: PMC557072.

49 Colorado Medical Treatment Decision Act of 2010, C.R.S. § 15-18-101, et seq.

50 MedlinePlus. Bethesda (MD): National Library of Medicine (US); Updated October 31, 2022, https://medlineplus.gov/ency/patientinstructions/000473.html.

51 Tanya D. Marsh, *The Law of Human Remains: When Dirt and Death Collide: Legal and Property Interests in Burial Places* (Probate & Prop., 2015).

52 "Reliance — Declarations." Colorado Revised Statutes, § 15-19-105, 2024.

53 Ted Godbout, "Wealth Transfers to Hit $84 Trillion Through 2045," National Association of Plan Advisors, January 24, 2022, https://www.napa-net.org/news/2022/1/wealth-transfers-hit-84-trillion-through-2045/.

54 "Will the 'Great Wealth Transfer' Transform the Markets?," *Merrill*, Bank of America Corporation, accessed May 5, 2026, https://www.ml.com/articles/great-wealth-transfer-impact.html.

55 "Lost Bitcoin Wallet Passwords Fuel Rise of Crypto Recovery Services." *Reuters*, distributed by EZ Newswire, September 30, 2025, https://www.reuters.com/press-releases/lost-bitcoin-wallet-passwords-crypto-recovery-services-2025-09-29/.

56 See Fiduciary Access to Digital Assets Act, Revised, accessed May 10, 2026, https://www.uniformlaws.org/.

57 "About Inactive Account Manager," Google, accessed May 10, 2026, https://support.google.com/accounts/answer/3036546?hl=en.

58 "Legacy Contacts," Facebook Help Center, accessed May 21, 2026, https://www.facebook.com/help/991335594313139/?helpref=related_articles.

59 "How to Add a Legacy Contact for Your Apple Account," April 02, 2026, https://support.apple.com/en-us/102631.

60 "About Memorialize Instagram Accounts," Meta, accessed May 10, 2026, https://help.instagram.com/231764660354188?helpref=faq_content.

61 "Memorialize or Close the Account of a Deceased Member," LinkedIn, accessed May 10, 2026, https://www.linkedin.com/help/linkedin/answer/a1336663/memorialize-or-close-the-account-of-a-deceased-member.

62 "How to Contact X About a Deceased Family Member's Account," X, accessed May 10, 2026, https://help.x.com/en/rules-and-policies/contact-x-about-a-deceased-family-members-account.

63 Craig Parker, "The Evolution of eWill Legislation," Trust & Will, 2023, updated March 21, 2025, https://trustandwill.com/learn/ewill-legislation.

64 See Electronic Wills Act and Electronic Estate Planning Documents Act; Uniform Law Commission, https://www.uniformlaws.org/.

65 "Remote Electronic Notarization," National Association of Secretaries of State, NASS, accessed May 5, 2026, www.nass.org/initiatives/remote-electronic-notarization.

66 Jones, "Estate Planning Statistics."

67 "Home." *My Life & Wishes*, accessed May 5, 2026, https://www.mylifeandwishes.com/.

68 "DocuBank." *DocuBank*, accessed May 5, 2026, https://www.docubank.com/.

69 "Everplans: All the Pieces of Your World in One Safe Place." *Everplans*, accessed May 5, 2026, https://www.everplans.com/.

70 "FidSafe: Secure Storage for What Matters." FidSafe, accessed May 5, 2026, https://www.fidsafe.com/.

71 Trustworthy: The Family Operating System®." Trustworthy, accessed May 5, 2026, https://www.trustworthy.com/.

72 "Home." LifeSite, accessed May 5, 2026, https://www.lifesite.co/.
73 "GoodTrust: Estate Planning Made Easy, Secure, and Affordable." GoodTrust, accessed May 5, 2026, https://mygoodtrust.com/.

Appendix E

Index

www.ingramcontent.com/pod-product-compliance
Lightning Source LLC
LaVergne TN
LVHW100140061126
851857LV00010B/172